Country Living

Country
Paint

Country Living

Country Paint

Traditional Decorative Paint Techniques

Text by

ELEANOR LEVIE and RHODA MURPHY

Foreword by

RACHEL NEWMAN

HEARST BOOKS

New York

ISBN: 0-688-15099-3

Printed in Singapore
First Edition
1 2 3 4 5 6 7 8 9 10

Text set in Minion

Art Director: Patti Ratchford
Designers: Patti Ratchford and Gretchen Mergenthaler
Editor: Camilla Crichton
Paint samples by Eleanor Levie

Produced by Smallwood and Stewart, Inc., New York City

Contents

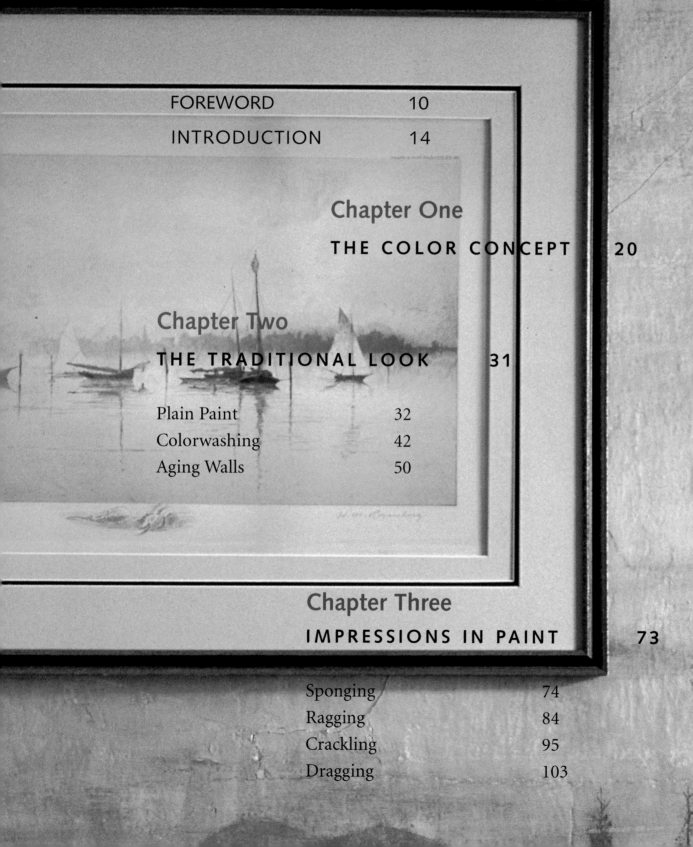

Chapter Four

DESIGNING WITH PAINT 115

Chapter Five

ARTISTRY WITH PAINT 149

Chapter Six

PREPARING TO PAINT 170

Foreword

COULD THERE BE A MORE PERFECT TOOL FOR THE COUNTRY DECORATOR THAN PAINT? I HAVE SEEN SO MANY DIFFERENT KINDS OF ROOMS—LARGE, SMALL, MODERN, OLD—TRANSFORMED BY PAINT THAT I am convinced it is the answer to any decorating woe. Whatever the look and feel you want—quiet, bold, bright, subdued—paint can accomplish it.

In this book you'll learn how to achieve wonderful effects with paint. The step-by-step instructions for a variety of paint techniques are accompanied by our own "color" swatches, which show alternative color choices and will help you make your decorating decisions. Some of the methods may be new to you, but their warm looks will be instantly familiar. From the earliest colonial times Americans have turned to paint to mask crumbling walls, add color to a room, and lend a decorative touch to a plain space. Paint can fool the eye. Aging walls, for example, can make a nondescript modern room look as though it has the grace of years. Other techniques can be called upon to highlight a room's qualities, or to make up for its shortcomings.

The versatility of paint is one reason I like it so much. It's a wonderful way to express artistic sensibilities, without making too much of a commitment. You can try out a new color in a corner of a room, or experiment on basecoated cardboard with a new technique—it costs little time or money to expand your paint horizons, and the results are stunning.

The one lesson about paint that I have learned in my travels is that anything goes. Wash, splatter, drag. Be creative with color. Forget the rules. Whatever you do, have fun. Pull on your old clothes, get out your paint brushes, and go to work transforming your home!

Rachel Newman, Editor-in-Chief

Introduction

Introduction

Likenesses on canvas, carriages painted, ornamented, gilt and varnished. Signs of all kinds. House and ship painting carried on. Paints mixt at short notice." In 1775, painter Abraham Delanoy was advertising his services in the *Connecticut Journal.* Delanoy was not unusually versatile for his time. Like most artisan painters, he was, by necessity, part color expert, part artist, and part chemist. He would follow recipes (or create his own) like those gathered by Hezekiah Reynolds in his *Directions for House and Ship Painting,* written in 1812, which suggested, for example, boiling red lead together with oil, then adding "one gill of Copal Varnish or Spirits of Turpentine," to make an interior oil paint. Delanoy's long apprenticeship would have taught him how to grind both exotic and mundane ingredients into pigments (colors) for mixing into paints, how to stencil, and how to create such elaborate decorative effects as faux marble or tortoiseshell.

In the colonies, a painter was a valued tradesman. The wondrous ability of paint to protect and beautify wooden surfaces made it precious in a society that relied heavily on wood for boats, homes, and furniture. For years, paint enabled the poor to imitate the furniture and decors of the wealthy—painters commonly copied the elaborate grain patterns of sought-after mahogany on to humble pine or maple furniture. Wood was also frequently painted to resemble costly stone—in 1705, for instance, part of the capitol at Williamsburg was ordered to be "painted like marble." And in the days when wallpaper was a rare commodity imported from France, paint permitted eighteenth-century Americans to mimic its patterns and colors on their walls.

Even today, paint remains indispensable. We still use it to copy fine wood, stone, and wallpaper. But, more importantly, to express our artistic sensibilities. Humble, relatively inexpensive, and readily available, paint is the most versatile of decorating tools. Its ability to bring color and pattern into a room at a reasonable price is unsurpassable. Think of all a couple of cans of paint and a few brushes can do: change a small dark space into a rich retreat, remake a white box room into an architectural masterpiece, transform a blank wall into a fantasyland, infuse a home with beautiful and brilliant hues. In a room that feels inhospitably large, paint can create intimacy. In a room with cracked and damaged plaster walls, paint can be used as clever camouflage.

Best of all, paint is the simplest way to fill a house with that most elusive and desirable of decorating traits—personality. We all want our homes to be unique, and paint is one of the few ways to make them truly distinctive. Unlike wallpaper or fabric, no two paint treatments are identical. Even if the colors are the same, one combed wall will never look exactly like another. The same holds true for a color-washed ceiling, or a stenciled chair. In a world of mass reproductions, the sense of being hand-done—with all its inevitable imperfections and character—is the very essence of a paint treatment's appeal. But, the limitless possibilities of paint—in terms of type, finish, color, and pattern—can make this seemingly simple material daunting. No one is immune to it. Most of us have at least once painted a room white simply because we couldn't decide what else to do. But after reading this book, you will see white as a color choice, not a fallback position.

Here we explore paint at its country best: from the warm, inviting textures of the "broken paint" techniques—sponging, ragging, crackling, dragging—to the charm of stencils and freehand expression, with an abundance of other looks in between. These are looks that don't require a pre-Revolution farmhouse to work. They can delight in any setting and on many surfaces—not just walls, but floors,

ceilings, trim, and furniture as well. Not only that, they are surprisingly easy to achieve, even for a novice. Clear, straightforward how-to instructions lead you by the hand. To simplify color decisions and spark the imagination, a page of color swatches accompanies most techniques. The final chapter will aid you in making sense of all the different paints, as well as the various paint products and tools you need to create the looks you want. We also teach you the basics of painting—from filling holes to painting bare wood.

So this book has several goals. First, to make you aware of the decorative opportunities provided by paint. Second, we want to help you make informed design choices that you will love. Third, to teach you how to execute those choices on your own, even if you've never picked up a paintbrush before. Above all, we'd like to free your imagination and give you the incentive to begin enriching your home.

Chapter One
The Color Concept

The Color Concept

WE OUGHT NOT TO BE TIMID ABOUT COLOR, FOR THE OLD TIMERS LOVED IT, BOLD AND BEAUTIFUL," WROTE ESTHER STEVENS BRAZER IN HER 1943 BOOK, *BASIC INSTRUCTIONS FOR HOME PAINTING IN the Early American Manner.* Wise as these words are, anyone who has ever shuffled through a sheaf of tiny rectangular paint chips can attest that choosing color is the toughest part of painting. Yet even while we curse those paint chips, we should count our blessings. It wasn't until the end of the nineteenth century, when commercially produced paint became widely available, that homeowners could tell beforehand what the final paint color would look like. Even the painter couldn't be sure until after he'd ground and mixed the pigment into the basic paint. (What we call "paint" really consists of two elements—the "base," which is the mixture that provides bulk and adhesion, and the "pigment," which provides the color.)

Every era has had its own ideas about color, and once in a while a period is defined by its colors. The 1970s, for example, are associated with Day-Glo orange, pink, and green, and with harvest gold and avocado green. In the Victorian age, deep burgundy, navy, and other somber hues were so pervasive, and room schemes were so busy, that Edith Wharton and architect Ogden Codman Jr. urged home-owners literally to lighten up. In their 1897 book *The Decoration of Houses,* they wrote that "each room should speak with but one voice: it should contain one color [preferably ivory or gray for the walls], which at once and unmistakably asserts its predominance..."

During the late eighteenth century, rich homeowners displayed their wealth with colorfully painted walls. George Washington's home, Mount Vernon, for example, was a riot of color—with rooms painted bright blue, green, and yellow.

The Wiseburg Inn, a structure in Parkton, Maryland dating from 1798, is an even better example. It featured a bright orange parlor, and a hallway painted verdigris, with a vibrant yellow dado and celery-hued woodwork. At that time, such vividly colored rooms were status symbols, not only because the owner could afford to pay for the paint and the painter, but could also buy the precious, and therefore very expensive, pigments that produced the desired colors.

Obviously then, the price of paint was determined by the pigments used to color it, which is why barns were usually painted red—the colorant, iron oxide, was readily available. Only the wealthy could have their rooms painted Prussian blue— its cerulean hue came from costly prussic acid. The sources of the other common pigments of the time sound like a virtual witches' brew. Carmine came from dried insects. Cobalt ore produced a distinctive shade of blue. Ultramarine was derived from lapis lazuli, a semiprecious stone. Copper ore made green. For different shades of yellow, the painter could either use saffron filaments, buckthorn berries, mercury, sulfur, or arsenic. The pigment for a black was called Collin's Earth and came from peat bogs near Cologne in Germany.

Interestingly, the muted blue-grays, mustards, and sage greens that are usually associated with the colonial period were actually either much darker or a brighter shade entirely when they were originally painted. Prussian blue is a particularly good example. For years experts believed that it was a soft green. But in fact the green came about as a result of chemical changes. Linseed oil, a frequently used ingredient in paint at that time, darkens and yellows when not exposed to sunlight, turning blue paint over time into green.

Today, there is an infinite number of color choices, which is both the good and the bad news. In addition to countless ready-mixed shades, paint stores and expert colorists can custom-mix any shade you like. Paints have been matched to many things—a green apple, a manila envelope (a favorite of many designers), even the color of a homeowner's eyes. Such an embarrassment of riches can be a curse in that it makes picking the right color so difficult.

Although most of us base our color decisions on instinct, there is a science to color. Called the color wheel, it was invented by Isaac Newton in the seventeenth century and is still in use today. All the primary (red, blue, and yellow), secondary (orange, purple, and green), and tertiary (all the shades in-between) colors have their place on the wheel. Colors opposite each other, say, red and green, are called complementary and when paired will bring drama to a room. Colors next to each other on the wheel are called analogous; green and blue, for example. Analogous colors harmonize well.

Much later, but equally important in impact, was the work of Frenchman Michel Eugene Chevreul, director of dyes for the Gobelins tapestry works. His 1839

treatise *The Principles of Harmony and Contrast of Color* (first published in English in 1854) explained how the pairing of various colors could alter their appearance. For example, he showed that a red placed beside an orange looks more purplish, while the orange color seems more yellowish. During the era of Darwin, Chevreul's color theories and laws of harmony influenced the Victorians greatly, and they are the primary reason why Victorian houses were painted in so many unusual colors. The color of both the interior and the exterior of a home was given great thought. But in those days homeowners had plenty of time to think—plaster walls often took up to a year to dry completely. Furthermore, there were many books and articles in circulation that outlined the "correct" colors for painting each room in the house, and even went on to explain how those colors should be combined.

Today, we know that there are certain immutable facts about color. First of all, colors do affect our moods. Studies have shown that hyperactive children are

calmer in rooms with cool colors—blues and greens—but will become agitated in spaces decorated with hot colors—yellows and reds. Second, we know that dark colors recede and light colors advance. In other words, a room painted midnight blue will feel smaller than one painted off-white. That doesn't mean that all small rooms must be painted light shades, and vice versa. You may want a tiny sitting room to have a cozy, enveloping air, or you may wish for the walls of a large living room to visually disappear. Third, dark colors absorb light and paler colors reflect it (which is, of course, why people wear white in the summer). If you want a room to feel bright and airy, opt for a pale color; to minimize the amount of light, choose an absorbent, darker hue.

These rules, however, are nothing more than guidelines, which all designers routinely ignore. For instance, the great decorator Billy Baldwin loved to use a deep chocolate brown for painting living rooms; he wanted to make them exceptionally dramatic at night. In other words, nothing is set in stone. The best colors for a room depend on so many factors—the type of room you are decorating, its mood, the time of day it's used, and above all, the personality of the people who live in it. In other words, color is a subjective, personal choice. And the right colors for your spaces are the ones you love.

plain paint

colorwashing

Chapter Two
The Traditional Look

aging walls

antiquing wood

PAINT CAN IMBUE ANY ROOM WITH A TRADITIONAL AIR.

CERTAIN COLORS CONVEY CLASSIC STYLE—THE DUSKY HUES

OF THE SO-CALLED WILLIAMSBURG SHADES, FOR EXAMPLE: THE DEEP

greens, the mustardy yellows, the soldier grays. Rooms painted with such shades speak of an earlier time even when bereft of furniture. But paint can also be manipulated to achieve the very same elegant antiquity—paint techniques such as colorwashing, aging, and antiquing deliberately mimic the patina of age.

In this chapter we examine these styles and the moods they create, from the beauty of solid blocks of deftly combined colors to the worn appeal of distressed surfaces. All these effects have a firm place in country style; they are the antithesis of slick and shiny, lending rooms a quiet and gentle beauty.

Each technique imparts a distinctly different image. With plain paint, carefully chosen colors harmonize to bring balance and interest to a room. There's no law, for example, that states all woodwork and ceilings be white, nor that all parts of a wall be the same shade. This look involves pairing different hues, and different paint finishes (see Chapter Six), to bring out each color's best qualities.

Colorwashing, on the other hand, brings subtle style to a space. The gentle variations of color that characterize this technique create the air of an ancient wall in Tuscany or a Scandinavian farmhouse. The aging walls technique produces another kind of rustic charm, as new surfaces are distressed to resemble old, crumbling plaster walls. Finally, antiquing wood transforms any wooden surface, even furniture, into well-worn relics.

The walls (opposite) have been painted using distemper, an old-fashioned paint that provides a deep, matte finish. Distemper is an ideal choice for covering uneven walls and is much favored for its desirable flat finish. Unfortunately distemper is toxic, which makes it a little a tricky to find. However, ordinary flat latex paint makes a good substitute—it has a similar finish and is much more durable.

Plain Paint

ECISIONS ABOUT PAINT AND PAINT COLORS HAVE VARIED THROUGHOUT HISTORY, DETERMINED BY THE CUSTOMS OF THE DAY. THROUGHOUT THE LATE EIGHTEENTH CENTURY, FOR EXAMPLE, convention decreed that a single color should be used to decorate whole rooms—and so it is uniformly painted woodwork that is colonial style's distinctive hallmark. By the late Victorian era, fixed rules and the day's fashionable wisdom were used to determine colors. Magazines and decorating books stated that ceilings must be painted the lightest color, walls a touch darker, and woodwork the darkest of all. Furthermore, homeowners were urged to choose coordinating colors from a somber palate: brown, maroon, green, for instance. Surprisingly, white wasn't used for painting ceilings or trim until the twentieth century.

While few of us want our rooms to be as dark and—to our eyes—as gloomy as the Victorians, think beyond white as your first color choice. A small room will feel larger if contrasts are minimized—with the ceiling, walls, and trim painted the same color, there is nothing to stop the eye and the room will appear bigger. Conversely, a more intimate air is created if you use a darker shade of the wall color for the ceiling. Contrast can be added by utilizing white or, even better, another color. Using combinations of colors will always give an individual style. Woodwork will stand out if you opt for a darker shade than the walls, or vice versa.

Meanwhile, your paint options are many. The various finishes, such as milk paint—its finish is reminiscent of velvet—or glaze, all impart differing looks and textures.

When opting for a sharp color contrast, as in this sitting room (right), keep the lines between the colors crisp. To paint this room, the tray ceiling was tackled first, then the painter used a slanted brush to cut in the turquoise paint at the top of the walls.

A popular Early American color, particularly for woodwork, was vibrant yellow (opposite). But a trim this vivid and shiny demands at least two coats of high gloss paint over a primer applied with a good quality bristle brush. For heavy-use areas such as kitchen cabinets and mantels, use durable oil-based paints.

A paint scheme derived from the original eighteenth-century colors allows a 1700s farmhouse to retain its vintage charm (previous page). The dark green woodwork provides a strong counterpoint to the much paler walls. The blue cupboard, neatly positioned in the space between two doorways, is almost as old as the house. Layers of paint were painstakingly scraped back to reveal the original coat of paint.

Look beyond ordinary latex and alkyd paints as covering choices. Glazes and traditional milk paint, though more likely to be found in craft rather than paint stores, imbue walls with distinctive style. Milk paint gives a natural finish to raw wood surfaces and its beauty can be seen in this restful annex (opposite), which is a new addition to a 175-year-old cabin. Here, the paint helps insure that the new room blends seamlessly with the rest of the house.

Glaze combines a pigment with a varnish or sealant to form a translucent topcoat. A light brown glaze applied to the walls lends an air of cozy relaxation and calm to this bedroom (above).

To give the green bathroom floor (above) the utmost durability, high gloss oil-based paint covers the floor, and is topped with multiple coats of varnish—providing the protection needed to keep scuff marks at bay. The same type of oil-based paint could also be used for the exterior of a bath tub. (Enamel paints and epoxy combinations are also available for reglazing the inside of a bath tub.)

To lend the wallboards of the bathroom (right) a weathered appearance, the homeowner first brushed them with white paint, followed by a dark stain—giving them the look of driftwood. The mirrors are bordered by salvaged window frames that were left just as they were found.

Color unites this open-plan galley kitchen (above) with an adjoining family room and eating area. To show off the grain and wood tone of the pine cabinets, as well as the island's bead-board panelling, the homeowner covered them with a single coat of blue-green milk paint. Natural beeswax is the ideal sealant for this type of surface—it will protect the wood and leave only the slightest sheen. Italian stone countertops complement the cabinetry.

The combination of light blue and dark blue brings interest and definition to ordinary, and otherwise unexciting, kitchen cabinetry (opposite). The blues also provide charming contrast to the yellow range, hood, and countertops. An extra coat of semigloss oil-based paint on the shelves keeps them unscathed as dishes and treasured collectibles are constantly removed and replaced (a clear varnish would also do).

An additional paint treatment, ragging (see Chapter Three), embellishes the walls and ceiling.

Colorwashing

EXECUTED IN WARM SHADES—SUCH AS ORANGE, YELLOW, PINK, OR RED—COLORWASHING EVOKES A SUN-DRENCHED AND RAIN-WASHED MEDITERRANEAN VILLA. WATERY BLUES AND GREENS, ON THE OTHER HAND,

call to mind a Swedish cottage. Like a veil of color, gently rippling over the surface of the wall, colorwashing brings quiet drama and elegance to a room. One of the most beautiful and sophisticated of paint treatments, it is also one of the easiest. It simply involves brushing either diluted paint or lightly tinted glaze over a basecoat to create a very subtle dappled effect.

For anyone new to decorative paint techniques, colorwashing is the most forgiving of all treatments; its characteristic flushes of color hide every mistake, just as they disguise the imperfections of a badly flawed or damaged wall. Colorwashing is also especially good for camouflaging the hard-textured walls so popular with developers during the 1970s.

As a surface for colorwashing, uneven plaster or drywall is a blessing in disguise. Flawed walls provide the perfect rough canvas for this technique. In a living room (opposite and right), the walls' dry matte finish suggests that old-fashioned distemper paints were used for the wash, when in fact modern paints were used. To get the ethereal blue-green, a tinted topcoat was brushed over a white basecoat. As an accent, the cabinetry and shelves were painted light blue. The bold red chair and upholstery colors pop out against this airy backdrop.

If you love strong colors, but worry they will overpower a room, try colorwashing. This technique will soften and subdue any hue—even the most vibrant. A pastel shade, therefore, becomes the barest hint of color.

In colorwashing, the subtlety or boldness of the brush strokes determines the character of the wall almost as much as the color. Depending upon how you wield the brush, the method's intrinsic mottling can be either understated or quite obvious.

Whatever your final decisions are, with colorwashing you can quickly and easily achieve country appeal, even in the most modern home.

Colorwashing mutes a vivid shade of red (previous page) to make it more palatable in a casual sitting room. Although pastels are the more generally preferred color-washing hues, this technique also works as a way of keeping strong colors restrained. Here, attractive, deeply hued walls brighten the space, but without overpowering the bold graphics or the informal furnishings.

Meanwhile, the fluctuating color of the wall (opposite), gives a dreamy quality to the room. Against such a watery-green background, the plain pine hutch and simple demitasse set look like objects in an old Scandinavian farmhouse.

Bolder brush strokes bring a lively pattern to a child's bedroom (above). The color, however, was carefully chosen for its serenity and acts as a counterpoint to the strong colorwashing. Plenty of white trim also helps to keep the walls in check.

Colorwashing

The colorwashing effect is designed to simulate an exterior wall where the original paint has faded and mottled over time—the color seems to float over the surface. A watery and primitive quality is desirable in the brushwork, and a large, soft bristle brush should be used to apply the topcoat lightly and in ever-changing directions. These quick, short strokes will often cross each other and some of the basecoat should still show through. While the resulting paint surface is very uneven, it should look balanced throughout, simulating the appearance of naturally aged walls.

In the top row of swatches shown here, a wash—paint thinned with water to the consistency of cream—was used for the topcoat. At top left, the basecoat is cream, washed over with bright yellow. At top center, a pale yellow wash was used, this time over a white basecoat. The final board, at top right, has a white basecoat. This was colorwashed with the same pale yellow, then again with the brighter yellow. Combining the two yellows in this way gives extra depth and intensity to the treatment.

A popular modern colorwashing technique utilizes water-based glazes—where a small amount of color is mixed with clear glaze. This results in a much more durable finish, with a slight shine. At bottom left, a cream basecoat is colorwashed with a yellow-gold glaze, while at bottom center an even warmer effect is achieved by using the same yellow-gold glaze over a yellow basecoat. Finally, at bottom right, a cream basecoat is colorwashed with clear glaze colored with just a little brown creating a very subtle, muted effect.

Aging Walls

SUNLIGHT, MOISTURE, THE DIRT AND GREASE FROM COUNTLESS FINGERTIPS, THE PROGRESS OF TIME, AND THE ENDLESS SHIFTING OF AN OLD HOUSE—THESE ARE THE ELEMENTS THAT CAUSE RIPPLES AND TEARS, AND ultimately give character to plaster walls. But you can imbue modern drywall surfaces with that same mystery and beauty solely with paint. The method of aging walls is really a series of complementary techniques. It can require carefully darkening a wall in specific places—such as edges and corners—or deliberately causing paint to not properly adhere in other areas, using touches of furniture wax paste; or rubbing off a topcoat with sandpaper to reveal the colors underneath, even the bare wall.

One of the joys of this method is the amount of creativity involved. There are no fixed patterns and you can add your decay wherever and however you wish. To keep genuine deterioration at bay, however, and to protect the paint, you should consider topping your treatment with a thin matte sealer.

In a world where new always seems to be better, leaving old, battered walls in their neglected state may seem like an act of heresy. But there is a very distinct beauty to faded, flaked, and darkened plaster walls. Whether they are the real thing or helped along with paint, aged walls evoke ancient ruins.

This living room (right) received only minor wall repairs—cracks were filled and a thin coat of paint was washed over the wall. Meanwhile, in the hall and bedroom (opposite) the homeowner removed 1950s wallpaper, then wisely left the plaster walls he found underneath untouched.

The color gradations of this effect are subtle and never jarring. It is a sophisticated look that evokes the faded beauty of English or French manor houses. When you use aging walls as a decorative jumping-off point, fabrics should be kept as muted as the walls. For window treatments, think of diaphanous sheers, country checks and stripes, or delicately printed cottons made into loosely constructed draperies. Equally, upholstery should be understated—choose faded chintzes, damasks, and solid hues for coverings that won't compete with the eye-catching walls.

In an old house, covering original walls with sleek, smooth drywall-compound is often inappropriate. Instead of hiding deteriorating walls, revel in them as the owner of this 1787 Cape (previous page) has done. He wanted his period house to be livable, but without compromising its integrity. So he left the original hand-lathered plaster walls and woodwork unembellished and free of any twentieth-century touches. To keep the walls in their present state, and to prevent any further decay, a coat of clear matte sealer is a sensible precaution.

After stripping the wallpaper from the master bedroom of this old house (left), a much more beautiful and subtle pattern was discovered. Remnants of the old paint remained and, combined with the cracks and patches of new plaster, the effect is truly country elegant. To complement the walls, the owners also partially stripped the mantel and chair rail of their paint. The result is a perfect back-drop for the Shaker boxes and eighteenth-century blanket chest.

How to Age Walls

Simulating the effects of decades of sunlight, moisture, and wear and tear is surprisingly quick and easy to do. And creating these artificial signs of aging will give even newly constructed walls all the appearances of an antique.

For realism, look at where the walls to be aged are located. Where a wall receives direct sunlight, sand down the paint, dulling and lightening the color as if direct sunlight has faded the area over the years. Moisture seeps into walls, particularly in kitchens and bathrooms, and causes paint to flake off. Rubbing furniture paste wax onto selected areas and then over-painting means that the paint will not adhere properly and can be easily flaked off. Also consider which areas would receive the most wear, and rub back the paint those places.

You can also darken the surface with tinted glaze to mimic the look of paint that has accumulated a buildup of grime over time. Take particular care over corners, crevices, and the recesses along moldings—the places where dirt and dust would naturally gather.

1 Prepare the surface to be aged, mask off adjacent surfaces, and apply the basecoat. Allow the basecoat to dry completely.

2 To flake the paint, use a flat artist's brush to dab areas of furniture paste wax or petroleum jelly onto the surface. Apply a single topcoat using a roller or with colorwashing brushwork (see page 49). So that the paint is easier to remove, let it dry only slightly before starting to distress.

3 Scrape with a paint scraper to remove those areas of the paint covering the furniture wax. Additionally, use coarse sandpaper to rub away the topcoat to reveal the underlying basecoat. Work particularly on the areas that receive direct sunlight.

4 Repeat steps 2 and 3 with a second topcoat in another color.

5 Finally, to mellow the look and simulate years of grime, use a foam brush to apply a clear glaze tinted with just a little burnt umber, dark brown, or black.

Notice the swirls of dark brown furniture wax on the detail above left—it is helpful if you make a "map" to remind you where the wax was laid. A tan color was applied here as the first topcoat. Above right, a light blue topcoat was then applied over the tan, and scraping and sanding has been partially completed.

Aging Walls

Any painted surface is subject to all sorts of wear and environmental effects, and the more you work at a surface—combining different techniques, such as scraping, sanding, flaking, scratching—the better your simulation of a well-distressed wall will be.

All of these examples of aged walls were executed with latex paints with eggshell finishes. At top left, a rich blue topcoat was darkened with a quick brushing of clear glaze tinted with medium brown. The same glaze was then used to lightly spatter the surface (see page 185). The taupe colored swatch beside it, at top center, was treated in the same way, using a clear glaze tinted with burnt umber.

The swatch at top right began with a taupe basecoat. Furniture paste wax was then applied, and topcoated with a rich blue. Next the surface was scraped and rubbed to flake and wear back the paint. Patches of plaster were added and extra cracks were created using a hammer, before a final sanding back to almost reveal the basecoat.

At bottom left a dark cherry-red topcoat was flaked and sanded to reveal a rich blue basecoat. The surface was then further distressed by throwing a bicycle chain against it. Finally, dark burnt umber paint was rubbed into the pitted areas. At bottom center, the basecoat is dark cherry, while the topcoat is rich blue. As before, the blue surface was flaked and sanded, then a dark burnt umber glaze was dragged over the surface to darken it (see page 108). At bottom right, some of the dark cherry topcoat was rubbed away, revealing a taupe basecoat. Patches of plaster were then added, and the surface was further sanded back.

Antiquing Wood

EVERY SO OFTEN ONE STUMBLES ACROSS A RARE PAINTED TRUNK, A HUTCH, A WINDSOR CHAIR—IT MAY EVEN BE IN A MUSEUM— THAT HAS BEEN ABANDONED TO THE HANDS OF TIME. OVER THE YEARS,

no one saw fit—or had a moment—to put a new coat of paint over its chipped and worn surface, and so the ages took their inevitable toll. Inside old houses, panelling, doors, and other wooden surfaces may also have remained untouched. There is a homey elegance and delicate beauty to such surfaces that always evoke a sense of wonder in the past and invite the touch of curious fingertips.

Happily, new or simply humdrum furniture, panelling, and woodwork can be given a hundred year's worth of patina in just a few hours of antiquing—the process of artfully applying a series of paints and glazes, usually darkly tinted, and then carefully distressing them to emulate the effects of time. Any wooden surface can gain charm and distinction from this effect, which instantly mellows new or not-so-new moldings, ordinary kitchen cupboards, or a dull and unremarkable piece of furniture.

The cupboard (right) is a genuine antique, and could have provided the inspiration for the kitchen (opposite). Some of the paint has flaked off, revealing an earlier stain—while patches of bare wood, scratches, and pitting are the signs of actual wear and prove its true age.

Even a new kitchen can gain an air of timeworn rusticity with careful antiquing. Modern and and unremarkable, the cabinets in this kitchen were coated in blue paint, which was then sanded off using vertical strokes. For added authenticity, the distressing was concentrated along the edges and around the door pulls.

The secret with antiquing is to strive to avoid uniformity—seek irregularity instead. When antiquing, concentrate your efforts to simulate wear and tear in the places that would have gotten the most use logically in a genuinely old piece—on the edges, corners, and bottoms of doors, around drawer pulls and handles, and so on. Conversely, allow the dark paint or glaze to collect in cracks and crevices, the places where dirt and grime would naturally have accumulated.

For a lover of old houses, there can be nothing more rewarding than painstakingly scraping away layers of paint and wallpaper and uncovering an original stencil or stain. For any decorative painter, these preserved painted surfaces provide inspiration and a model to imitate in modern schemes.

The owner of this house in Texas, dating from 1896 (above and opposite), scrubbed off one hundred year's worth of soot and grime, only to discover a treasure trove of nineteenth-century paint treatments.

The original German owners had painted the bedroom walls white—then added dark green below to mimic woodwork. Finally a traditional German pattern was stenciled around the top of the wall.

The newly cleaned entryway, meanwhile, revealed a painted and pattern-stenciled ceiling and more faux-painted baseboards.

Clearly, the family who first lived in this house were rich in imagination and cleverly used paint to simulate the trappings of the rich in brilliant and jewellike colors. We can reproduce these stunning effects in our homes today, simply by painting and stenciling, then gently rubbing back the paint with rough grade sandpaper; wearing right back to the wood in a few places.

Traces of eighteenth-century aquamarine milk paint illuminate the cracks and crevices of the doors and panelled walls in this early house in Massachusetts (left). The homeowners restored the back hall as closely as they could to its original condition— removing layers of paint until they reached the earliest coating. The room beyond is a new addition, built and decorated to blend with the old house. In particular, the floor was stained with milk paint.

The original two-tone ochre and brown paint on the door (above), and even the wood, has worn away over time. Scratches, scraping, pitting, and flaking, all combine to create a truly distressed appearance.

How to Antique Wood

Like aging walls, this is a subtractive technique. Antiquing wood is specially designed to give wooden surfaces—such as moldings, window frames, panelled doors, cabinets—a timeworn appearance. It can also be used to good effect to provide a centuries-old look for the simulated wood used in many homes for crown molding.

For this technique, use a colored glaze, or a clear glaze that's been colored. This glaze is brushed onto the surface, and then immediately wiped off with another brush. For a look of faded grandeur, use a metallic tint to color the glaze, such as the Old World bronze used here. Gold, copper, or silver could also be used to produce a look of elegant decadence.

For a more rustic look, burnt umber, burnt sienna, brown, or black will work well. And don't stop at simply wiping off glaze. Sand back and strip away paint as well. You can further elaborate the distressing by utilizing the methods suggested for aging walls, and you could also consider incorporating a little crackling (see page 95).

1 Prepare the area to be antiqued, mask off adjacent surfaces, and apply the basecoat. Allow the basecoat to dry completely.

2 Prepare the glaze. If you are mixing paints or tints into a clear glaze, be sure to stir the mixture thoroughly. Also, stir it intermittently as you work, so that it does not separate.

3 To apply and wipe the glaze, it's best if two people work together (unless the area to be worked is small). The first person should use a foam brush to apply the glaze in the direction of the wood grain.

4 The second person should wipe off the glaze, immediately after application. Use a stiff bristle brush, and pull it through the glaze, also following the grain. Most of the glaze should be removed, leaving behind only fine, directional lines. Make sure that the glaze fills depressions and crevices—where it would not have worn away so easily over time. Wipe the brush often to keep the bristles almost dry. To insure there are no obvious breaks, go back a couple of inches each time to overlap with previously worked areas.

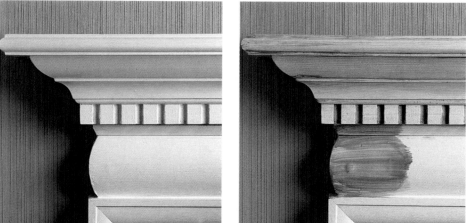

Here a simple white basecoat was applied to a mantel and then topcoated with a clear glaze colored with Old World bronze in a ratio of four to one (a good ratio for antiquing effects). Notice how heavy the application of the glaze should be prior to wiping off, above right.

Antiquing Wood

Aging walls and antiquing wood are both techniques with which you can create the character, distinction, and warmth of a historic home, even in the most modern of homes. With antiquing wood, adding glaze then wiping it away while it is still wet is the easiest way to acquire a well-worn look.

On the swatch at top left the basecoat was a very bright red. Then a burnt umber glaze was brushed on and wiped off. Afterwards, the same glaze was used to speckle (see page 185) the surface, adding richness and depth. Directly below, at bottom left, the swatch began with a more sub-dued, dark red basecoat. To create the look of faded glory, a mixture of clear glaze and Old World bronze was applied as the topcoat.

In the center, both swatches started with realistic wood tones. A light brown stain covered the sample at top center. Furniture paste wax was rubbed over in places, so that the topcoat, in this case a red glaze, would not adhere in those areas when applied. A gentle sanding back reveals the natural wood tone where the wax was positioned. At bottom center, the board was treated with a golden oak stain for the basecoat, then brushed lightly with copper and wiped.

Finally, at top right, a natural wood stain basecoat was topcoated with Old World bronze–tinted glaze, then speckled with burnt umber glaze. Below, at bottom right, a red stain (this could also be done with barn-red milk paint) was applied for the basecoat. The topcoat is a copper glaze that was brushed on and wiped so that all but a few highlights were removed.

dragging

crackling

sponging

Chapter Three
Impressions in Paint

ragging

PAINT TREATMENTS WORK IN DIFFERENT WAYS. IN SOME,

SUCH AS AGING AND ANTIQUING, PAINT IS MANIPULATED

TO ATTAIN A DELIBERATELY DISTRESSED EFFECT. IN OTHERS—

sponging, ragging, crackling, and dragging, which are the treatments explored in this chapter—it is the tool used and the manner of the paint application that determines the effect. These are the so-called "broken paint" techniques, where the paint is applied and then immediately removed. (In the case of ragging and sponging, the paint can also be applied with an applicator tool other than a brush.) The tool used—a bunched-up rag, a crumpled paper bag, a large sea sponge, a special dragging brush, a piece of cardboard— creates the individuality and character of the effects.

Ragging produces the look of softly crumpled silk, while the delicate lines of dragging bring quiet depth to walls and woodwork. The gentle mottling of sponging introduces a variety of colors into a space and crackling, which recreates the network of fine lines that so often appear on older painted pieces, is literally the result of paint breaking.

The popularity of these techniques stems from the fact that they look wonderful and give surfaces a rare three-dimensional appearance. These are effects that yield patterns that are so subtle, you shouldn't be surprised if visitors reach out and touch the walls to see if they aren't papered. Indeed some of these effects were developed in the early eighteenth century to simulate expensive wallpapers imported from Europe. Ironically, there are now wallcoverings that are designed to mimic these very same techniques! But mass-produced wallpaper can never capture the charming, purposeful irregularity of the real thing.

This dining room's tricolor wall treatment (opposite) was inspired by the mottled tortoiseshell glaze of coveted nineteenth-century Rockingham pottery. Gold, rust, and chocolate-brown paint were applied one after the other with scrunched-up rags. Attention is kept focused on the walls and art-work, by keeping the furnishings country simple and the oversize windows unadorned.

Sponging

O F ALL THE DECORATIVE PAINT TECHNIQUES, SPONGING IS PROBABLY ONE OF THE MOST REWARDING FOR A BEGINNER. BLISSFULLY EASY, THE TECHNIQUE REQUIRES VIRTUALLY NO ARTISTIC

talent—not even a steady hand—and it gives beautiful results. The faint dappling of sponging brings a quiet depth and pattern to a room, and allows the subtle introduction of different colors—as many colors as you like can be sponged on top of one another. You can also use different types of sponge to create a variety of looks, and your technique with the sponge can be in pounces that are close together, overlapping, or far apart.

A few tips to remember. Generally, it is sea sponges that produce the most pleasing effects; however, regular cellulose sponges can also be used with good results. When you are applying the paint, touch the wall only lightly with the sponge—otherwise, if there's too much paint, or if you press too hard, you'll be left with a blobby mess rather than the delicate pattern you seek. Practice on pieces of basecoated cardboard before you begin— that way you can refine your technique and determine your colors.

When it comes to choosing your colors, it's best to select colors that are similar in tone; be aware that the last color you apply will be the most prominent.

Finally, depending upon the sponge you choose, the technique you use to apply the paint, and the colors you pick, you can use sponging to simulate stone or aged walls— try using this treatment in tandem with the aging walls techniques: sanding, flaking, scratching, etc.

In the open-plan living and dining room (opposite) of this converted granary, which dates from the 1850s, sponging has been used to cleverly simulate the appearance of stone—a light beige wash was sponged over a white base. The furnishings were kept generously sized and simple, so that they don't disappear into the large and lofty space—the ceiling is twenty-six-feet high.

The stairway of this Maine home (right) combines both ragging and sponging. First the walls were rag-rolled. Then, in lieu of a stair runner, the stair risers were sponged with light brown on top of a dark brown basecoat.

A light aquamarine sponged over a deeper basecoat brings to mind the cool colors of the ocean, and bathes this potentially dark attic room (previous page) in a flood of light. The sea and fishing are the keynotes in this relaxing, masculine retreat—collections of decoys and fishing-themed postcards decorate the walls.

Though cramped, a city galley kitchen is a welcoming spot (opposite), thanks in part to yellow walls sponged with a taupe glaze. The bright walls impart country style and keep the space sunny, even on dreary days. To maximize storage, the owner has covered one wall with perforated pegboard to keep utensils within easy reach.

The owner of this weekend retreat (above) had only one goal when it came to the decoration of his newly built house: to give it "disheveled and traditional character." He accomplished this by sponging the dining room walls to resemble well-aged plaster. They provide the ideal rustic backdrop for a varied collection of folk art furnishings and collectibles, which includes a 1950s oak cow propped upon the windowsill.

How to Sponge

ponged walls often allude to the pointillist paintings of the French Impressionists. The blues and greens shown on the following page may bring to mind a lush garden, a glistening body of water, or a copper roof weathered to a verdigris patina. Opposite, a sky blue basecoat was over-sponged with pale blue and just a little soft white. The result gives the wall the aura of a sunny day—high cirrus clouds float across the sky and it's not hard to imagine a gentle breeze stirring the miniature windmill.

To create this effect, a natural sea sponge was used, but any kind of sponge can be used for sponging. A cellulose kitchen sponge, for example, will give a more open web of paint (but cut this type of sponge into an irregular, rounded shape to avoid harsh lines).

With sponging, there are no hard and fast rules, only many possibilities. For a soft, mottled texture, sponge over the basecoat while it is still wet; or sponge over an already sponged surface—before it has time to dry—with a wet sponge, or stipple (see page 185) with a soft brush. Over-sponging with another color will add complexity.

1 Prepare the area to be sponged, mask off adjacent surfaces, and apply the basecoat. Allow the basecoat to dry completely.

2 Pour about ¼ cup paint for sponging into a paint tray and thin the paint to the consistency of cream—use water for water-based paints, and mineral spirits for oil-based paints. To sponge two colors together at the same time, pour a small amount of the second color into the tray and mix together just a small amount.

3 To sponge, first dampen the sponge to soften it. Then dip the sponge into the paint; if you are using two colors, pick up a hint of the second color as well. Blot away excess paint on newspaper and, using a light, up-and-down motion, pounce the sponge against the wall. With a minimum of overlapping, continue pouncing adjacent areas, turning the sponge slightly each time, so that you achieve uneven repeats of the lacy pattern. Strive for a random, but balanced, overall texture.

4 To sponge into corners, use a small wedge cut from the sponge, or you can dip an artist's brush into the paint and dab into the inside angle to mimic the mottled effect.

A sky blue basecoat is over-sponged with pale blue and a little soft white (above and opposite).

Sponging

With sponging, it is the choice of sponge and paint that determines the effect. A sea sponge nearly dry of paint, for example, gives a crisp texture to the lacy web of color; while a thinned-down paint or glaze produces a soft, mottled appearance. All the samples shown here began with a latex basecoat in an eggshell finish.

At top left, a sea sponge mitt was used to sponge a taupe basecoat with a blue glaze mixed with a clear glaze (in a ratio of one to four). At top center, the same glaze mixture was applied with a sea sponge over a cream basecoat. Both swatches show how sponging with a glaze creates a light, translucent effect where the base color shows through the glaze as well as through the negative spaces that sponging leaves behind.

When you use opaque paints, however, be careful not to overwork the sponging, or the top color will conceal too much of the color underneath. At top right, the basecoat is light cream over-sponged with two colors: first blue, then green. At bottom left, the same colors were used in reverse order, this time over a taupe basecoat. On both occasions, a kitchen sponge was used.

At bottom center and bottom right both swatches were basecoated in a rich blue. At center, a sea sponge was dipped into green paint and blotted onto newspaper to remove most of the paint. Because so little paint was left on the sponge, the resulting pattern is light and lacy. The swatch at bottom right shows sponging off, rather than on—a green glaze was brushed quickly over the basecoat with a foam brush, then immediately sponged off with a sea sponge mitt.

Ragging

WHAT COULD BE MORE SIMPLE THAN BUNCHING UP AN OLD RAG AND DABBING IT OVER A FRESHLY PAINTED WALL? THAT'S ALL RAGGING REALLY IS. PERHAPS IT BEGAN AS A POOR MAN'S MARBLING, TO imitate fabric wallcoverings, or maybe a painter trying to correct a mistake discovered a charming new texture—regardless of its development, ragging is undeniably pleasing. Its telltale blurred appearance gently injects pattern into a decor.

There are many versions of ragging—in the first, which is similar to sponging, the paint is pounced onto the wall with a balled-up rag. In the second, wet paint brushed onto the wall, then blotted off with a wadded rag. Then there is rag-rolling, where a twisted rag is used either to roll paint onto the wall, or to roll wet paint off. In each of these variations the effect is obvious, and so ragging always looks its best if the basecoat and topcoat are tonally similar.

When you are selecting a rag to apply or remove the paint, it's wise to experiment on pieces of basecoated cardboard until you find a texture that will give you the effect you are looking for. Try old sheets, cotton T-shirts, chamois cloths, etc. But don't confine yourself solely to textiles: try paper bags, paper towels, or plastic wrap. The possibilities are almost endless. Obviously, you should use the same type of material for a whole project, otherwise your ragged walls won't have a consistent appearance.

One word of warning: rags soaked in oil-based paints are a fire hazard, so don't throw them out until they are thoroughly dry.

A ragged finish brings beauty to an undistinguished mantel (right). First, the soft beige-painted wood was daubed with a rag dipped in white paint, then a few well-spaced pounces of aquamarine followed.

In the bedroom (opposite) tan and pumpkin-toned milk paint were ragged onto newly plastered walls with terry cloth rags. The result is such a haven of tranquil peace that the homeowner often retreats to the room and uses it as a temporary studio.

It's hard to believe, but this kitchen (left) is newly created, although the room that houses it (originally a bedroom) is old. Rescued pine furniture and open shelving, displaying the owner's collection of old pans and china, give the room an old-world atmosphere—as does the new range that is designed to look vintage. Luckily, it fitted perfectly into the room's original fireplace. But it is the stripped wooden floor and the rag-daubed walls that really give the room its historic feel. The warm appearance of old parchment comes from topping an off-white basecoat with first a taupe glaze, then a yellow one.

Ragged walls introduce a sense of romance to the sitting room of a colonial-era house (left), a feeling that is enhanced by the handsome furniture—in particular the fainting couch, which is a treasure from the attic. The finely mottled wall texture makes a simple stenciled frieze look not only ancient, but sophisticated and elegant.

This airy living room (above) is a calm and soothing place to be. The owner originally painted the walls and panels plain white, but soon found them too glaring and uninteresting. To improve their look, he rag-painted them with an ecru color. As a result, the walls have an intriguingly mottled appearance and a mellow glow that resembles faded plaster.

How to Rag

Ragging will either produce a subtle and indistinct patterned effect, a randomly distressed appearance, or a strong textured look. Everything depends upon the colors, the applicator material, and the paint types that are used.

Clearly, the combination of basecoat and topcoat colors produce a myriad of possibilities. Whether the topcoat is an opaque paint or a translucent glaze stretches the horizons still further. But with ragging, there are also countless materials to use as the applicator, and the texture of the fabric affects the result. A rag from a cotton-knit T-shirt, a coarse weave or waffle-weave fabric, terry cloth, chamois, felt—and that's just the beginning. What about paper and plastics? They can be wadded up as well; further expanding the range of results.

To create the effect shown opposite, two coats of paint in rosy red were applied, then over-ragged with a tinted glaze. The glaze was created by first mixing together equal measures of black cherry and black glazes. Then one part of this mixture was mixed with four parts dark bronze and eight parts clear glaze.

1 Prepare the area to be ragged, mask off adjacent surfaces, and apply the basecoat. Allow the basecoat to dry completely.

2 Prepare the paint or glaze. If you're mixing colors, or mixing paint or tint with a glaze, transfer the mixture to a squeezable container. This means that you can frequently shake the container and keep the colors well blended while you work. Squeeze a small amount of the mixture into a paint tray as and when you need it.

3 To rag, select a rag about 12-inches square and dampen it slightly to soften it (if it's fabric). Pull on a pair of rubber gloves, then wad the rag in your hand, turning under the corners and raw edges. Dip the rag into the paint. Apply the paint to the wall, patting quickly and vigorously. Make the first few dabs very light, so that the paint-soaked rag will not leave heavy globs of color on the wall. You can go over these areas again when the rag is no longer leaving much paint on the surface. Strive for an even texture throughout.

4 To rag into corners and tight spaces, wad up a 4-inch square of rag and dab gently into the angle.

A ragging mitt, available in craft stores, was used to apply the topcoat (above and opposite).

Ragging

The variations that can be achieved with ragging are endless. Not only is the range of applicator material virtually limitless, but you can also rag off as well as rag on. To rag on, the topcoat is applied with the wadded or twisted (a little or a lot) applicator by pouncing or rolling over the surface, either horizontally, vertically, diagonally, or in combination. To rag off, the topcoat is brushed on as normal, but then immediately removed with the chosen ragging material, again by pouncing or rolling. When ragging off, be sure to work quickly—so either do small areas at a time or work with a partner.

Left are some of these possibilities. For the swatch at top left, a twisted rag, dipped in pale green glaze, was rolled vertically down a surface that had been basecoated in cream. At top center, rag-rolling was also used but this time with a dark green glaze over a light green basecoat. At top right, a cream basecoat was brushed with light green glaze and immediately blotted with a wadded ball of terry cloth toweling to rag off some of the glaze.

At bottom left, wadded cellophane wrap was used to apply dark green glaze over a light green basecoat. Next, at bottom center, cream paint was ragged onto a light green basecoat using a loosely wadded paper towel.

Finally, at bottom right, a light green basecoat was quickly brushed over with a dark green glaze. Immediately afterward, the glaze was ragged off using a mop mitt. (Mop mitts are available at craft stores, although you could use a section of a string mop to produce the same finely mottled result just as effectively.)

Crackling

WITH TEMPERATURE AND HUMIDITY CONSTANTLY SHIFTING, MOISTURE GRADUALLY SEEPS IN BETWEEN THE LAYERS OF PAINT OR VARNISH ON AN ANTIQUE OIL PAINTING OR PIECE OF FURNITURE, AND A WEB

of hairline cracks appears over time. The same thing can also happen to painted wood surfaces: mantels, panelling, doors, windowsills, etc. These appealing mosaics of cracks are true indicators of age, but by using paint and a special crackling medium, you can create just the same appearance in no time at all—occasionally, the appearance of the cracks is almost instantaneous.

The art of crackling takes advantage of a chemical reaction between the medium and the topcoat—where the topcoat is caused to shrink as it dries, cracking as it does so. Just be aware, when you use the crackling technique, that you'll have very little control over the cracks that appear—chemistry is at work, not the hand of the decorator. You can choose your colors and where the cracks will appear, but that's about all.

Depending upon the colors you select, the look can be authentically natural—a dark brown basecoat with an off-white topcoat, for instance—or dramatic—a deep purple undercoat, say, with bright red on top.

This is an excellent effect to incorporate into an aging and antiquing scheme. When you are antiquing wood, apply the crackling medium before you apply the topcoat, then begin your sanding down and wearing back once the cracks have appeared and the topcoat is fully dry. Your wood surfaces will be imbued with extra eye-catching charm.

A network of alligator cracks brings understated interest to the flat boards of this kitchen's woodwork (opposite). To simulate this humble and well-worn effect, first apply barn-red paint, then the crackling medium. Finally, apply a topcoat in blue. To complete the look, distress the topcoat with a little light sanding, then protect and preserve your work with two or three coats of sealant.

An old set of drawers (left) contributes a romantic air to this bathroom. The chest's creamy-white topcoat has a series of emphatically large cracks, which reveal a dark stained basecoat.

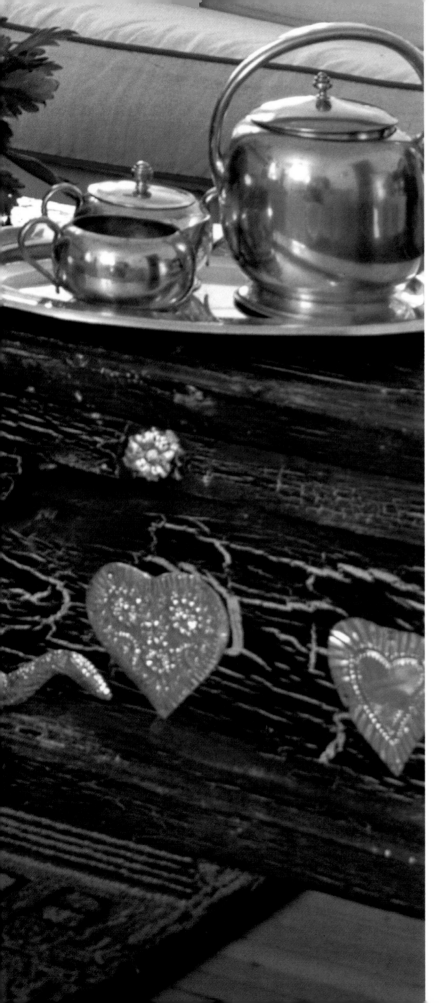

With crackling you can really experiment and have fun with dazzling color combinations.

The choice of paint colors and the use of crackling medium, for example, turn this whimsical trunk into a work of art (left). To create this finish, a metallic silver paint was used for the basecoat, then covered with crackling medium. Purplish blue and navy paints—not properly blended together on a palette—were then applied using heavy brush strokes in a mostly horizontal direction. (The orientation of the brush strokes can, to some extent, influence the direction of the resultant cracks.)

The chest was then further embellished with hammered tin hearts, flower studs, and snakes. Short, turned legs illuminated with the same silver paint raise the trunk to coffee-table proportions.

How to Crackle

Crackling is a technique where you have to relinquish much of the control: chemistry takes over, and the effects are always unique.

To a limited extent, you can exert some control over the cracks by the way in which you paint. The direction in which you brush on the topcoat usually determines the direction, and therefore the appearance, of the resulting cracks—so if you brush mostly in a horizontal direction, your cracks will have a predominently horizontal orientation.

As a general rule, if bold and dramatic cracks are what you are looking for, select a topcoat color that contrasts with the basecoat color. If you want to achieve large cracks, apply the topcoat thickly and in ever changing directions. A fine web of cracks can be achieved by using a sea sponge—gently touching the surface, making sure to cover all the spaces.

Crackling medium (see page 176) is water-based, so you need to use water-based paints for the topcoat. The type of paint used for the basecoat is of little importance, but if you are applying the basecoat choose water-based paints.

1 Prepare the area to be crackled, mask off adjacent surfaces, and apply the basecoat. Allow the basecoat to dry completely.

2 Apply the crackling medium as you would regular paint. Flat-finish basecoats will require a slightly heavier application than eggshell or semigloss, because they tend to be more absorbent. Apply the medium evenly for a consistently crackled appearance; unevenly if you just want to crackle sections. Allow to dry for no longer than 45 minutes to an hour, until just tacky to the touch.

3 Working quickly, apply the topcoat. Try to avoid brushing over an area twice, and always brush into the applied area, rather than working out from it.

4 Finally, 2 or 3 coats of clear varnish should be applied to high-use surfaces. (It is not necessary to varnish infrequently touched surfaces.) Crackling treatments take up to 30 days to fully dry, so do not place objects on a crackled surface until the full month is up.

Above and opposite, a light orange basecoat was randomly sponged with red acrylic craft paint, so that the cracks would be slightly variegated. The crackling medium was then applied, followed by a brushing of bright blue semigloss latex.

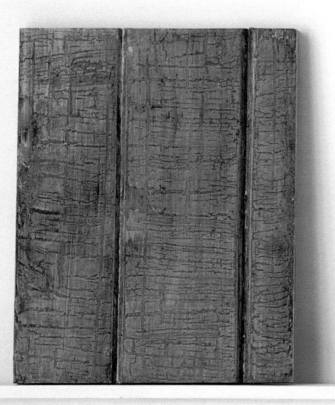
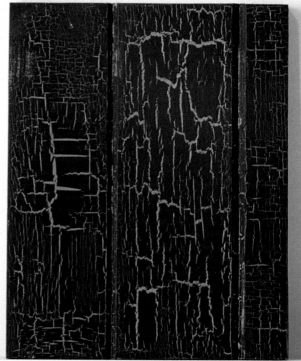

Crackling

Crackling is an excellent way to give wood the worn patina of age, and is a wonderful enhancement to other distressing techniques.

At top left, the crackling technique has been used to age the white basecoat. The topcoat is a clear water-based glaze that was brushed on after the crackling medium. Then, an "antiquing glaze" was rubbed over the surface using a sea sponge. The antiquing glaze sinks into the cracks, giving them definition and the appearance of antiquity. (Antiquing glaze is available at craft stores.) At bottom left the basecoat is again clearly visible. Here it is tan, but in this case a clear glaze tinted with burnt umber (in effect, homemade antiquing glaze) was rubbed into the cracks.

At top center, metallic copper paint forms the topcoat, and was applied with horizontal strokes over the crackling medium and a cream basecoat. At bottom center, dark burnt umber was applied in vertical strokes over a metallic copper basecoat. In both, the cracks have a slightly more organized and regulated appearance than they would if the topcoat had been applied randomly. At top right, the application was random: the variety of patterns in the cracks is the result of constantly changing the direction of the brush strokes when the topcoat was applied over the crackling medium. The basecoat here is brown and the topcoat is cream.

Finally, a metallic glaze, Old World bronze, was used for the basecoat at bottom right. After the crackle coat, white paint was applied with horizontal strokes. The subtle golden glints the cracks reveal hint at sophistication, suggesting old money and aristocratic forebears.

Dragging

ACCORDING TO DECORATING DESIGN LEGEND, THE GREAT ENGLISH DECORATOR JOHN FOWLER POPULARIZED DRAGGING IN THE 1930S WHEN HE CREATED THE ENGLISH COUNTRY LOOK THAT HE MADE FAMOUS.

Actually the technique originated in the early eighteenth century as a quick way to simulate wood graining, which was otherwise a time-consuming paint technique. Later in the same century, decorative painters started dragging with colors other than wood tones so that they could mimic the expensive new wallpapers being imported from France.

While most decorative painting, such as sponging and colorwashing, makes rooms feel informal and rustic, dragging is suited to formal decorating as well as country style. The result it yields is elegant and sophisticated, making it ideal for bringing faint texture to woodwork as well as walls. Typically, dragging is characterized by fine pinstripes, but variations include cross-hatching, wavy lines, and other linear patterns. These lines, however, make it important that dragging—and its variant, combing—be done on surfaces that are completely smooth, because any irregularities will disrupt the lines and become more obvious.

Although dragging is simple enough in theory—you drag a special brush, a rubber combing device, or even an implement as humble as a corncob, through wet paint to reveal the color beneath—keeping the lines straight can be difficult. Be certain to apply pressure evenly and don't stop between strokes. If you want the dragging to stand out, pick contrasting colors. To make the outcome more subtle, opt for hues that are similar.

Stripes couldn't be more straightforward to paint on any surface with evident boarding—you simply use the boards as guides. That's how the red and green stripes in this festive kitchen were executed (opposite and left). To allow the wood grain to show through, the paint was applied to raw wood. Immediately afterward, the wet paint was dragged to remove much of the paint. With the addition of bright red trim and forest green curtains, the result is a kitchen that is the happiest and most cheerful room in the house.

Extraordinary as it may seem, the house that contains this dining room (previous page) was actually built in the 1960s, not the late seventeenth century as the decor suggests. A wonderful textural quality has been imparted to the room's panelling—by rolling a corncob through rust-colored paint applied over the original mustard basecoat. Meanwhile, the single-drawer Swedish cabinet has been gorgeously painted in a freehand effect.

A Shaker-style basketweave design in apricot paint over white serves as a bright backdrop for a bedroom that's joyously filled with Caribbean colors (right). To achieve this style, the peachy hue was stroked over the white basecoat, then combed in a cross-hatch fashion that echoes the webbing of the bed's head and footboard.

How to Drag

Dragging is a paint technique that was much in vogue during the eighteenth century—the fine striations with their subtle tonal differences provided an elegant look for those who couldn't afford expensive wallpapers. Today, a dragged wall is still just as sophisticated and attractive. However, it's tricky to achieve long striations that are even and straight, and so the technique takes a little practice. Nevertheless, there is no harm in a few small imperfections in the finish—they serve only to create a homespun country look, and add to the graceful charm of the effect.

When dragging, confine yourself to flat surfaces without molding or texture. If you work on a small, contained area, such as the back wall of a shelf unit, below a chair rail, or along stair risers, one person can handle the job. However, dragging over large areas is a two-person job, since the topcoat may start to dry before it can be dragged effectively. For this reason, it's best if you use slow-drying oil-based paints.

Be sure to use a lightly colored basecoat with a little sheen, such as semigloss, then the darker topcoat won't be absorbed.

1 Prepare the area to be dragged, mask off adjacent areas, and apply the basecoat. Allow the basecoat to dry completely.

2 Prepare your topcoat paint or glaze. If you are creating your own color, mix it well, and prevent the mixture from separating by stirring it occasionally as you work.

3 Brush on the topcoat. Apply from top to bottom in one 3-foot-wide section at a time. If you are working with a partner, one person brushes on, while the second person drags.

4 The topcoat should be dragged immediately after application. Starting at the top, drag the dragging tool through the topcoat to the bottom, without lifting from the surface. After each drag, wipe the tool. Make sure adjacent sections overlap, so there are no breaks in the dragged lines. The objective is an evenly striated surface.

5 Repeat steps 3 and 4 until you have completed the area.

A light pink semigloss was used for the basecoat (above and opposite) while the topcoat is a deep rose. The dragging tool was a four-inch wide stiff bristle brush.

Dragging

The classic dragging tool is a four-inch wide, stiff bristle brush, but many other tools can be utilized to produce all sorts of different effects. Brushes and rubber combing tools in various shapes and sizes are commercially available, but you could also try nylon pads, steel wool, and metal mesh pads, which will all give a primitive scratchy texture to the surface. Whatever you use, it takes practice to sustain straight lines down—or across—a wall. Compromising by making irregular lines, wavy lines, or random, broken lines, will be rewarded with a charming country look.

At top left, a blue basecoat was brushed with a beige glaze, then vertically dragged with a graduated comb. At bottom left, the colors were reversed and the same comb was pulled through the wet glaze vertically, then horizontally.

The swatch at top center was basecoated in beige, then topcoated with blue glaze. This was quickly stippled (see page 185) with a stiff bristle brush. Wavy lines were then dragged through, leaving stippled spaces in between. The tool was a 3 x 5-inch piece of cardboard, with the short ends cut with pinking shears for dragging.

At bottom center, a blue basecoat was topped with a light brown glaze. A standard combing tool was pulled in straight lines, then again in undulating lines, creating a dazzling, moiré effect. At top right, the blue glaze, over a light brown basecoat, was also dragged with a standard comb: first horizontally, then vertically, at even intervals. At bottom right, a beige glaze was brushed over blue. A standard comb was dragged in alternating horizontal and vertical lines so that a basketweave pattern emerges.

Chapter Four
Designing with Paint

striping

stenciling

checkering

reverse stenciling

THE INSTINCT TO BRING BEAUTY TO ONE'S HOME IS UNIVERSAL. IT

IS A DESIRE THAT HAS FOR CENTURIES COMPELLED PEOPLE OF

MODERATE MEANS TO TURN TO PAINT FOR ITS ABILITY TO MIMIC

decorative materials that were either impossible to obtain or prohibitively expensive. In particular it was country folk who resorted to paint to copy the decorative adornments of the wealthy. They used stenciling, for example, to re-create fine woodwork and costly inlays on furniture, and they painted their floors or made floorcloths to simulate fine carpets, oriental rugs, marble mosaics, and parquet.

For these people, lack of funds was never a hinderance; it was simply fuel for their imaginations. Today the paint techniques they developed—stenciling, striping, and checkering—are valued as decorative arts in their own right. This is not just because they are beautiful, but because of their ability to amend the shortcomings of a space—a stencil around a ceiling will compensate for a lack of molding, boldly checking a floor will disguise aged and faded wood, and a striped wall will make a low ceiling appear higher.

In addition, these paint techniques are always striking, and always get noticed. Over the course of this book, we've looked at many treatments whose charm emanates from the irregularity of their design. Their appeal is in their imperfection and unpredictability. But distinct, repeating patterns, such as those covered in this chapter, evoke different delights. Unlike the understated and subtle patterns of, say, sponging and ragging, these command the eye instantly. Even when they are executed in light colors, checks, stripes, and stencils demand attention, making them ideal for creating unforgettable rooms.

You can dramatically alter the appearance of a wood floor by painting it with a geometric design, such as in this entranceway (opposite). Here a partially checkered pattern in gray and white has been used around the room's circumference. The design has been boldly painted with hand-mixed milk paint and gives the room an injection of truly traditional country charm.

Striping

WITH THEIR AFFINITY FOR PATTERNS AND STRONG COLORS, THE VICTORIANS LOVED STRIPES, AND IT WAS DURING THEIR ERA THAT STRIPES BECAME FASHIONABLY POPULAR FOR DECORATING WALLS.

Classically elegant and wonderfully stylish, stripes can imbue a space with both of these desirable qualities. They can be bold and full of gusto, with bright and sharply contrasting colors, or they can be quietly noticeable, serenely painted in two very similar shades. Stripes can also be dressed up by combining them with other paint treatments or by mixing paint finishes. For example, one color stripe could be ragged, while the other is left plain, or one color could be painted in a high gloss paint while the alternate is executed in a flatter finish.

Stripes play visual tricks on the eyes. Beware, for example, of narrow stripes, which can give a busy appearance—so be careful to paint them in tone on tone, or to limit them to a single wall in an open foyer or to a space well broken up by doors and windows.

The ideal stripe width for your room depends upon its size and the height of the ceiling—stripes three to five inches wide are good standard widths that suit most spaces. As a general rule, the larger the space, the more stripes it can handle. Remember that stripe-painted walls can make the room's ceiling feel higher—so if the ceiling is already ten feet or more, stripes will telescope the room and make it look too long and narrow. In some cases, such as in the room opposite, painting the molding a strong color will cap the stripes and minimize this effect.

The mix of paint techniques in this bedroom (right and opposite) gives the stripes an extra fillip of style. First a cream basecoat was applied to the wall, then the stripes were taped. The blue-green color was then sponged on between the lines of tape. The striking effect brings traditional elegance to a room filled with Arts and Crafts–style furnishings. The owners have completed the look by staining the molding and French doors a deep brown that serves to accentuate the stripes even further.

Rather than painting a solid block of color in their hallway (previous page), the homeowners decided upon a strong two-tone stripe—in creamy yellow and yellowy pink: a color combination you'd be hard pushed to find in a wallpaper pattern book. Because the space is ample, they were able to use wide, confident stripes. To break up the expanse, and add a delightful, playful touch, they also painted a bright blue "runner" up the stairs.

A striped floor can subtly manipulate one's steps. In this soothing living room (left), the elegant white-and-gray stripes lead visitors into the room and right up to the most comfortable seating. In another space, a striped floor can dictate traffic patterns, or help to provide a smooth flow between rooms. A word of caution, however: stripes make rooms appear narrower than they actually are, so avoid them in long skinny areas—or paint them across the width.

How to Stripe

When it comes to striping, most of the work is in the preparation and measuring. Be very careful to thoroughly plan out your pattern for the stripes before you begin. Decide whether the stripes will be horizontal or vertical, what their width will be, if they will be evenly spaced or irregular, and whether or not the pattern will repeat. Carefully measure the space to be painted, determining how the stripes will be positioned.

Begin marking the stripes in the middle of a wall (or floor) and work out from that point. Also think about colors. Will you use more than two colors? Will they be tonal variations of the same shade, or will they be contrasting?

For painting the stripes, use a foam brush and apply the paint in only vertical, or only horizontal, strokes to match the orientation of your stripes. Here, just one coat of paint was used, which leaves thin striations where the basecoat just shows through. If you want a more solid stripe, apply a second coat immediately after the first coat has dried. It's best to work quickly, so that the tape can be removed promptly.

1   Prepare the area to be striped, mask off adjacent surfaces, and apply the basecoat. Allow the basecoat to dry completely.

2   Using a metal yardstick, a spirit level, and a pencil, mark the stripe positions with small, light dashes or dots. Mark the top of each stripe, the bottom of each stripe, and 12-inch intervals in between.

3   Apply painter's tape between the marks, to mask off the sections that won't be painted. As you apply the tape, pull it taut so it forms a straight line connecting the dots. Use a craft knife to cut the tape at the top and bottom. If you are striping a large area, you can do a few stripes at a time and reuse the tape. Burnish the tape by rubbing your thumb firmly along the edges to assure a good seal.

4   Paint the exposed areas. After each stripe is painted remove the tape, peeling it slowly off the wall and away from the wet paint.

5   Continue applying tape and painting the stripes until done. Erase any visible pencil marks and use a fine artist's brush to touch up any areas as necessary.

Use a lighter color for the basecoat and paint the stripes in a darker color. Here (above and opposite), a pale blue was striped with a darker shade.

Checkering

EUROPEAN COLONISTS INTRODUCED THE ANCIENT GAME OF CHECKERS TO AMERICA DURING THE SEVENTEENTH CENTURY, AND TODAY WE CONSIDER THE CHECKERBOARD PATTERN QUINTESSENTIALLY AMERICAN.

The pattern has been used so often as a decorating design that it is now an intrinsic part of our country folklore. Checkers can be found just about anywhere: on floors, walls, and fabric—though their usual home in terms of paint is on the floor.

The trick to successful checkering is in choosing squares that are the right size. When you are preparing to paint a floor, remember that too many checks can become dizzying: like stripes, checkers play tricks on the eyes. You can visually enlarge a small space by painting large checks—eight by eight inches is a standard tile size that works well. Or you can visually shrink a more cavernous space by using smaller checks—six by six inches or four by four inches are two common tile sizes. If you feel that an overall floor pattern may be too much, consider limiting the checks to a carpet-size rectangle—or paint an imaginary floorcloth.

As with all paint techniques, of course, your color options abound. For a traditional checkerboard look use red and black, or to imitate a marble floor go with the classic black and white. In fact, any color combined with white can't fail to look charming.

Finally, think about lending your checkered floor a venerable appearance by using a distressing technique (see Chapter Two) and, as always with painted floors, be certain to protect your work from damage with several coats of clear varnish.

Putting squares at an angle to the wall adds movement to a room (right). These oversize shapes measure eighteen inches square, and because there are so few in the pattern, they don't overwhelm the space. Painted in archetypal black and red, the checkers are enhanced by a stenciled border.

Checkers needn't just be the preserve of floors. In this peaceful bathroom (opposite), two soft shades of yellow were combined to create graceful checkers. After taping, the second color was sponged on, resulting in a lacy appearance which subtly complements the gossamer-thin curtains at bath and window.

A vivid red-and-white check along a ceiling cleverly substitutes for more elaborate architectural details and gives a bedroom almost all the pattern it needs (previous page). A few tricks can make a checkered ceiling border easy. First, ensure the top line of the border is even by running tape along the bottom edge of the molding or the ceiling edge if no molding exists. Start the pattern on the bottom edge of the tape and use squares cut from self-adhesive vinyl to mask off the alternate checks.

Once a forgotten outbuilding, this cozy cottage is now a snug home office (above). When he was converting it, the homeowner knew that a highly durable floor was a must. First, he basecoated the pine floor with a double coat of white paint, then he gridded the expanse into one-foot squares and painted every second square black, creating a graphic and classic checkerboard pattern. The final touch was to apply several coats of varnish to ensure complete protection for the floor.

A navy-and-white diamond-patterned floor forms the anchor for a decorating scheme in this welcoming breakfast/sitting room (opposite). Although checkers on their own add drama to a room, they can unobtrusively provide a pleasing backdrop for rugs.

How to Checker

Checkering floors has long been an inexpensive way to dress up plain and humble floors; but the technique is equally effective and attractive when used to decorate walls. As with striping, the key to successful checkering is in the preparation and measuring. Study the area you want to checker and decide what the orientation will be (diagonal, or horizontal and vertical), the size of the squares, and the colors you want to use, contrasting or tonal variations of the same shade. When you begin to mark out your design, be sure to start in the center of the area to be painted and work out from that point. Just as you do with striping, apply the palest color first, then use the darker color.

For a timeworn country look, you can also consider sanding back the paint to reveal the layers underneath, or perhaps even the wood or wall beneath. (Do this before you apply the sealant if you've painted a floor.) Study the sections on aging walls and antiquing wood in Chapter Two for some additional ideas you could incorporate.

1 Prepare the area to be checkered, mask off adjacent surfaces, and apply the basecoat. Allow the basecoat to dry completely.

2 Using a metal yardstick, a spirit level (if you are working on a vertical surface), and a pencil, mark the checkerboard pattern. A clear quilter's square or T square is essential for ensuring 90° angles. If the pattern is diagonal, a right angle triangle or protractor is invaluable.

3 Measure and cut squares from self-adhesive vinyl, and adhere the squares to mask off the areas that won't be painted. Burnish the edges by rubbing the edges firmly with your thumb. To prevent paint from seeping under the vinyl squares, paint the edges with a clear, matte sealer, or spray a clear sealer over the areas. Allow to dry completely.

4 Apply 2 coats of topcoat. Allow the first coat to dry before adding the second. When the final coat is completely dry, remove the squares.

5 If you've been painting a floor, apply 3 coats of sealer to ensure that the surface is durable. (You may need to reapply yearly.)

Painted floorcloths are the linoleum of yesteryear and you can easily make a floorcloth, such as this one (above and opposite), using the techniques described above. Use gessoed canvas, which you can purchase at any good art supply store.

Stenciling

FOR CENTURIES, PEOPLE HAVE USED STENCILS TO REPEAT A PAINTED PATTERN. FIRST INTRODUCED INTO EUROPE FROM CHINA IN THE SIXTH CENTURY, STENCILING WAS WIDELY USED DURING THE MIDDLE AGES FOR

decorating both churches and castles. For a while, stenciling fell out of favor, but it became popular once again in eighteenth-century Europe, and it was during this time that settlers began bringing the craft to the colonies. In America, stenciling thrived and developed into the folk-craft that we associate so strongly with our colonial past.

Today we continue to prize stenciling for its sheer versatility. Stencils can do much more than simply beautify a room—they can create an overall design, outline a particular feature, or disguise architectural defects. If a wall is too high for the proportions of a room, for instance, stenciled borders painted at the top and at the bottom will visually shrink the wall; and if a ceiling feels too low, a border stenciled around the inside edge of the ceiling will give the walls the appearance of height. Additionally, stencils can enliven spaces where

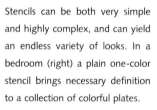

Stencils can be both very simple and highly complex, and can yield an endless variety of looks. In a bedroom (right) a plain one-color stencil brings necessary definition to a collection of colorful plates.

Meanwhile, the entrance to a conservatory (opposite) is marked by an intricate one-of-a-kind design. The artist responsible for this stencil-painted plant, tailored the design to the space and the realistic coloration of the leaves comes from carefully combining different shades of green.

detail is lacking—dull kitchen cupboards, for example, can be improved with stencils, or attention can be drawn to a lovely view by outlining a window with a stenciled motif. Whether you choose a design that is simple or complex, stenciling will always provide plenty of scope for creativity.

Traditional stencil designs are readily available (see Resources on page 188) but it's also easy to custom-make your own designs; and that way your stencil patterns will fit exactly into your decor. Study tiles, wallpaper, ceramics, fabrics, etc.—they are all good sources of inspiration.

Although this bedroom (previous page) is part of a new house, the room has a venerable aura due in large part to the stenciling that adorns the walls. The homeowner utilized traditional stencils for a singular design that conveys farmhouse flavor even in a house that's a mere five years old. She purposely chose muted nineteenth-century colors for the patterns, so that the stenciling looks naturally aged. Another option would have been to artificially antique the stenciling with a colored glaze.

Like any strong design element, you can plan your stenciling either to be the focal point of the room or an integral part of the design, as in this keeping room (above). With colors this playful, a lively stencil just adds to the fun and although there seems to be a lot going on, there's a method to the madness that keeps the busyness at bay—apart from the sten-

cils, the room is pattern free and there is plenty of white space between the stencils.

Combining stencils with free-hand effects (see Chapter Five) creates unique and wonderfully original designs. This dining room (opposite) has been given a romantic and whimsical air by over-painting the simple stenciled repeats with freehand effects. The look is completed by the gauzy window treatments.

How to Stencil

You can apply stencils to just about any painted surface—using just about any kind of paint; all you need to do is make sure the paint you use for stenciling is a little thicker than usual. You can do this just by allowing the paints to sit for a few minutes before you start applying them, so that some of the liquid can evaporate.

There is a multitude of places you can look for inspiration for your stencil design. Consider wallpaper designs, tile patterns, designs in magazines and pattern books, and so on. Take full advantage of modern technologies, such as computer graphics programs and photocopiers, to manipulate and refine your designs.

Milk paints, mixed to a pastelike consistency, were used (above and opposite) for this example.

1 Prepare the area to be stenciled, mask off adjacent surfaces, and apply the basecoat. Allow the basecoat to dry completely.

2 Sketch or trace your design or drawing, and then refine it, concentrating on the outline of the positive shapes—those areas that will be painted. Place a sheet of clear acetate or mylar over the completed design and trace, using a fine-tip permanent marker. Transfer the acetate sheet to a cutting mat and, using a craft knife with a fresh blade, carefully cut out the stencil. Always cut toward you and rotate the acetate as necessary.

3 To affix the stencil, first apply a spray adhesive to the back of the acetate and leave to set for a few minutes, until it is tacky to the touch —this will give you a temporary bond. Position the stencil on the surface to be stenciled and press down the cut edges firmly.

4 Apply the paint with a stencil brush, or your index finger wrapped with a 4-inch square of velour fabric. Dip the applicator into the paint and remove any excess by pouncing on paper towel or newspaper, so that the applicator is fairly dry. Then, starting at the edges of the cutout, and working toward the center, apply the paint by pouncing with the applicator.

5 To repeat the pattern, allow the paint to dry until just tacky and then carefully lift off the stencil and reapply in another location. Although one acetate stencil is all that's needed, duplicates will speed up the process.

6 For more complex designs using more than one color, each additional color should be applied individually. Cut a separate stencil for each color and allow the previous color to dry thoroughly before aligning and stenciling with the next color.

Reverse Stenciling

REVERSE STENCILING IS AN INTRIGUING TECHNIQUE THAT, AS ITS NAME IMPLIES, IS THE OPPOSITE OF STENCILING AND OFFERS A VERY DIFFERENT LOOK. INSTEAD OF PAINTING THE INSIDE OF A DESIGN, AS you do with regular stenciling, with reverse stenciling it is the outside of a design that is painted. Usually reserved for large areas where the reverse stencils are randomly scattered, this effect can also be used in the same manner as ordinary stenciling—as a border to create a false dado, for example, or to frame a door or window. Don't expect too much drama, however; reverse stenciling is an understated look that tends to be most effective where the colors are close in tone. Reverse stenciling looks wonderful when executed in plain paint, but it's more usually used in combination with other decorative paint techniques, such as dragging and sponging.

This treatment is best suited to simple images. Try a mix of different flat shapes that appeal to you: leaves, flowers, stars, crescent moons, or geometrics—triangles, diamonds, spirals, and the like. Other options might include borrowing a motif from wallpaper, greeting cards, fabrics, or patterned carpets. In fact, anything with a strong shape could be a candidate for transferring to a reverse stenciling pattern.

To temporarily adhere the stencils to the surface being decorated, use self-adhesive vinyl or a spray-on adhesive (available from craft stores). Allow the adhesive to dry for a few minutes before applying the stencils— then they will adhere during painting but will be easy to remove when you're done.

In this garden retreat (opposite) a faux-stone floor was created at a fraction of the cost of the real thing. First, the stone-colored basecoat was ragged on. Next irregular paving-stone shapes were stuck down. Grout-colored paint was then applied in the spaces between the shapes, which were peeled away when the paint had dried, revealing the "stones" beneath.

Reverse stenciling can also be used to produce delicate designs such as the imaginative treatment decorating this door frame (left). Here the yellow and black frame looks stunning against the red-painted wall.

Two lovers of nature brought the outdoors indoors quite literally, with a delightful reverse stenciling motif in their kitchen and dining room (left and above). For their design inspiration, they looked no further than their own garden.

To create this effect, they sprayed the backs of fern fronds and small broad leaves with adhesive spray, then pressed them onto walls which had already been basecoated and sponged. They then over-sponged the whole surface in another color, before removing the leaves.

How to Reverse Stencil

This technique allows you to cover a much larger area than ordinary stenciling. You have the option of either scattering your shapes randomly over a space, or clustering them together in attractive groupings. Bear in mind that the simpler the design, the more effective the result will be; and when you are refining your design, remember that with reverse stenciling it is not the interior of the shape that will be painted, but the exterior.

The technique works best if you also keep the colors restrained—especially when you are incorporating other paint techniques, such as sponging (see previous page) and ragging (as shown right and opposite). In both of these examples three colors were used: first the basecoat, then the second color was sponged or ragged on. Next the reverse stencils were positioned and affixed to the wall, and finally, the third color was added, again by sponging or ragging on. If you want to use just two colors, apply the reverse stencils after the basecoat, then apply the topcoat.

1 Prepare the area to be reverse stenciled, mask off adjacent surfaces, and apply the basecoat. Allow the basecoat to dry completely.

2 If you are incorporating another paint technique—ragging, sponging, dragging, and colorwashing all work beautifully—apply the second color now.

3 Sketch or trace your design or drawing, and then refine it, concentrating on the outline of the negative shapes—those areas that will not be painted. Trace your completed motif onto the back of self-adhesive vinyl. Do this several times, so that you have more than one reverse stencil to work with. Cut out the shapes. Consider making an inside cut-out using a craft knife, piercing the shapes with a hole punch, or cutting an edge with pinking shears. Peel away the paper backing and affix the shapes on the surface as desired.

4 Apply the topcoat or third color treatment. Allow the topcoat to dry completely, then remove the reverse stencils.

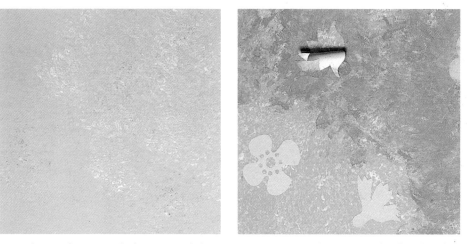

Here (above and opposite) the basecoat is a light gray. Using a mop mitt, this was ragged with a clear glaze that was colored with an equal amount of cream. After the reverse stencils were affixed, a darker gray glaze was ragged on—this time a scrunched up piece of terry cloth toweling was the applicator.

Chapter Five
Artistry with Paint

freehand effects

murals

W

HETHER YOU CHOOSE TO ADORN YOUR ROOMS

WITH MURALS, OR TO BRIGHTEN YOUR LIVING

SPACE WITH EBULLIENT DASHES OF COLOR AND PATTERN, YOU ARE

limited only by your imagination. When it comes to artistry with paint, there are no rules. All you really need is courage to accompany your creativity—and a strong dose of confidence to do something bold. What you don't need is the ability of a skilled artist. And you can take heart from the fact that your own efforts—more than anything else—make your home a true reflection of you.

Seek your inspiration from many fronts. You could borrow a design and colors from a favorite artist—Henri Matisse, for example, or Paul Gauguin. You could leaf through your favorite illustrated books, or look at magazines, greeting cards, postcards, and photographs for ideas. Or you might have memories of a much-loved view from your childhood that you want to preserve in paint.

You can limit your artistry to small spaces and paint a collection of surprises—a vine covered with flowers curving around a window, for instance, or a faux-painted ribbon and key by the door—or you may want to turn a blank wall into a focal point with a pastoral vista. The key with mural painting and freehand effects is never to be timid. Look beyond walls for paintable surfaces: doors, cabinet fronts, window moldings, ceilings, and floors are all perfect for your artistry. Whatever you decide to do, remember that so long as you follow your creative instincts, and work with confidence and panache, such paint treatments—however naive—inevitably pack a strong decorating punch.

In lieu of a blank space, a walled-up fireplace has been artfully used to express a love of old porcelain (opposite). Painted to resemble decoupage, the images are slightly flawed on purpose—they are not intended to fool the eye, only to amuse. Models for painting were not hard to find; the owner copied her own collection, pieces of which are displayed on the mantel and in front of the fireplace.

Freehand Effects

THE VERY ESSENCE OF CREATIVITY, FREEHAND EFFECTS HAVE NO RULES OR REQUIREMENTS TO HAMPER THEM; AND WHAT COULD BE MORE FUN THAN BRUSHING YOUR FAVORITE DREAMS, COLORS, AND images onto your walls—in whatever manner you like: dashes, dots, squiggles, stipples, spatters, drawings, and so on? Freehand effects produce an organic whimsey, that is always totally original to the creator.

The equipment that's needed is minimal (and you'll need just the same for mural painting). The most important thing is to have a selection of brushes. Artist's brushes are best, and they are usually sold in economical sets that include a variety of shapes and sizes. For most types of freehand painting, three types of brushes are essential. You'll require a round tapered brush to create both points and fat curves. A flat brush is also needed—they are great for filling in large areas, especially if you are working coloring-book style: outlin-

ing a design and then coloring it in. Finally, you'll need a fine liner brush for delicate lines. You'll probably find that you put all three to good use. Let's say, for example, that you are painting a sunflower. The flat brush is ideal for painting the big center, the round tapered brush for the petals and stem, and the fine liner for tendrils and highlighting fine details. Also useful is a fan brush, which is perfect for feathery effects and shading.

Your paint choices vary. Using up left-over interior house paint is just fine. But even better are artist's acrylics and craft paints that come in handy little tubes and bottles—and in countless hues.

Spattering takes no talent, yet it is rewarding and undeniably fun. A humdrum vinyl kitchen floor (opposite) is revitalized with lively spatters of marigold, blue, and cream. To spatter, simply drip on color by waving a stick or a brush loaded with paint. Just be sure to protect any adjacent surfaces!

Color reigns supreme in this carefree cottage (left). Even the banister is embellished with sassy colors and childlike patterns. The small scale of the designs keeps them from overwhelming the space. While this artist used acrylic paint and brushes, felt-tip markers that emit acrylic paint, called paint pens, make such doodling easy.

Since the Murphy beds and tables in the children's room of this vacation home tuck into the wall for extra daytime space, the walls were unavailable for hanging art. No matter—pictures painted directly onto the walls and woodwork set the scene in this room and never fail to delight the young occupants. Books on Native American art provided all the inspiration that was needed, and the primitive style of the work fits the informal room perfectly. In a casual space such as this, you could even let the children try their hand at helping to decorate—it will be an endless source of pride.

A square piece of cut-up sponge, dipped in moss-green paint and wielded with abandonment, turned a bathroom into a leafy bower (opposite), where to all appearances fronds of ivy freely range. For a more defined image, you could also cut an ivy-leaf shape from a special flattened sponge—the kind that expands after its first wetting. Or, try the new decorator foam stamps, available in a variety of shapes from craft stores.

A more mottled effect takes over a vintage bathtub in another bathroom (above). For the floor, the artist marked off checkers and dabbed a sponge randomly within the squares, using different colors at will. The panels of the door were also treated—this time to a simple, graphic pattern in uncomplicated primary colors.

Nothing gives a room a bigger injection of personal style than freehand painting; each treatment is different and inimitable. This sitting room is indeed one of a kind (previous page). Gaily painted ornamentations embellish just about every surface, yet the room doesn't feel overwhelming. The secret? Strong solid colors are left to the door and window frames, and the background wall color has been kept light. In addition, the images are all small and widely scattered.

The same exuberant spirit prevails in the kitchen (above), which illustrates clearly how bold shots of color, clever use of fabric, and a fun paint treatment can update a room inexpensively. With such vibrant hues, the painting has been carefully restrained.

The attractive painted carpet in this dining room (opposite) is unusual in that it is oval—more commonly, paint-decorated floors are rectangular in shape, and painted in stripes or checkers. The loose sprays of flowers and rippling interior border help to give the impression, at first glance, that this is a real rug.

THERE IS SOMETHING ABOUT MURALS THAT PLEASES EVERYONE. AS ANYBODY WHO'S EVER DRIVEN THROUGH A CROWDED CITY CAN ATTEST, THERE'S A THRILL THAT COMES FROM SUDDENLY SPYING A concrete wall transformed into a pastoral scene. Perhaps we are so fond of them because murals have been with us for all human time—after all, how else could one describe the ancient cave paintings of our prehistoric forebears?

Confidence and a little artistic ability help with mural painting. When you are deciding upon a picture, scale is crucial to bear in mind. If the painting will be seen from close range, then small images will work. But if it will be viewed from a distance, the picture needs to be large. A common mistake is to make a mural painting too small—so it is swallowed up by an expanse of wall. To help get the scale right, enlarge the picture you're using on a copier, then grid both the picture and the wall to scale. You can then copy the picture onto the wall using chalk or pencil. Even better, if you are able to get your hands on a projector (the kind that elementary schools use), you will be able to shrink and enlarge the image at will—and project it directly onto the wall space; then all you need to do is mark it straight onto the wall.

When your mural is planned and you are ready to get started with paint, practice on basecoated cardboard until you feel comfortable with the image and the paints. Additionally, it's best to use oil-based paints—they are slower drying than water-based paints, which will leave you much more time for manipulating colors and blending.

When the new owners of an 1860 Wisconsin home set about restoring the structure, they found this delightful mural (opposite) under layers of decades-old yellowed shellac. They later discovered that it had been commissioned in 1932 by a former owner as a means of illustrating the idyllic countryside of his youth.

Paint works wonders (left) to rectify an unsightly view out of a kitchen window. Tired of staring at a dispiriting blank wall, the owners of this city apartment painted blue sky and a lovely tree onto the wall—which both improved their kitchen and gave them a much more cheery outlook.

An airy summer-house boudoir, blessed with French doors that open out into a garden, gains an al fresco mood solely with paint (left and below). For the floor, the decorative artist created the look of flagstones simply by painting on irregular shapes in blue-gray paint. Hand-done vines and other small painterly touches complete the treatment and never fail to amuse the owner.

A cloud-strewn ceiling further blurs the line between indoors and out. Such sunny skies couldn't be easier to paint—simply coat the ceiling with a blue background, then use either a brush or a sponge to lightly dab on wisps of white for clouds.

Children's rooms are immensely satisfying to paint—the recipients of your labors tend to be pleased with any effort just as long as it's bright and colorful. A bedroom became a magical retreat thanks to a mother's imagination (previous page). When tackling their bedrooms, always remember how much children adore strong colors. If you allow them to pick the color scheme and motifs, it will make their rooms feel more their own. To make the decor last as long as possible, steer them away from popular images—such as cartoon characters—that they will quickly outgrow.

Take your inspiration from anywhere, just as long as it is meaningful to you. In this dining room (above) a Revolutionary War battle scene provides an appropriate decorative theme for a collector of early Americana. The colorwashed background helps to soften the drawing and makes it surprisingly peaceful.

In a bathroom (opposite) careful shading and mottling is the key to a landscape that calls to mind the great Depression-era murals. Too primitive to fool the eye into thinking this is actually a vista, the painting has the same calming effect in the room as a scene from a picture window might have. Notice how the colors get lighter higher up in the mural, to create a sense of distance. Keep in mind that when you are mural-painting in a bathroom, you should use oil-based paints, which are able to withstand humidity and dampness.

Chapter Six
Preparing to Paint

The Two Main Paint Types

For interior painting, there are two kinds of paint to choose from: water-based paints or oil-based paints. The general rule, when you select and buy your paints, is to use only water-based, or only oil-based, products throughout a decorating project. The different chemical compositions of the two types may cause problems—such as topcoat shrinkage or separation from the undercoats—if they are used together.

Don't worry too much about this, however. If you are moving, for example, and want to redecorate your new home to suit your own taste and personality, you can happily get to work with a can or two of the paint of your choice. Just bear in mind, when you are painting over an existing treatment, that you might need to use a primer (see page opposite and 179) to "neutralize" the surface before adding further coats of paint.

Water-based Paint

Usually known as latex paint, this type of paint is ideal for new and inexperienced decorators. Easy to apply and fast to dry, latex paints are also simple to clean up: brushes, tools, and drips on your skin can all be washed clean with a little soap and water. (Wash drips on fabric immediately with water; even dry cleaners will have problems getting dry latex paint off textiles. Use turpentine instead of water for oil-based paints—although, unfortunately, this type of paint is virtually impossible to remove completely.) The biggest benefit, however, is that latex paint is extremely versatile. Not only can you use it for both basecoating and topcoating but, so long as you use a latex paint with a flat finish (see page 180), you can often apply it as a primer as well. The matte flat finishes of today's latex paints come closest to matching the look of old-fashioned milk paint, distemper, and limewash.

Oil-based Paint

Compared to latex paints, oil-based paints (which are also called alkyd paints) are more expensive. They have the big advantage, however, of being silkier in texture and a lot more durable. Alkyd paints are more impervious to scratches, which make them a good choice for wood surfaces such as shelves and doors that are subject to considerable wear and tear. They are also the best choice for painting floors and in areas where there is a lot of moisture; using an alkyd paint in kitchens and bathrooms with poor ventilation, for example, is essential.

The disadvantage of alkyd paints is that they are not nearly so convenient as latex to work with, and it's harder to correct mistakes. Drying times are slow, which results in a longer wait between steps, and turpentine or mineral spirits are needed for cleaning up afterward. For best results, always use natural bristle brushes. A separate oil-based primer may also be necessary. Finally bear in mind, when choosing alkyd paints over latex paints for a project where either would do, that alkyd paints have a strong smell when wet that many people find unpleasant. (It also tends to linger.) Insure that you have good ventilation when you use oil-based paints, as the fumes can cause dizziness, headaches, and nausea.

Paint Finishes

Primers

A coat of primer is usually the first coat that you apply when you are decorating. You won't always need to use a primer; for example, if you are painting a darker color over an already-painted surface that has a flat finish. However, you will need to use a primer when you are painting surfaces that have never been painted, where you are over-painting a darker color with a lighter color, or where a wall has been patched.

A primer has a very flat, matte finish that is slightly rough. This roughness assists the adhesion of subsequent coats of paint and also improves the opaqueness and density of the final color. It is useful to have the primer colored to approximate the color of the next coat of paint. Always use an oil-based primer for alkyd paints, and a water-based primer for latex paints.

Flat Finish

Available in both water-based and oil-based versions, these paints are devoid of shine, absorb light, and exude warmth; they make excellent choices for flawed and uneven surfaces. They are especially good for ceilings and for areas of light use: living rooms, dining rooms, adult bedrooms. Because they can't be scrubbed clean, don't use these finishes in areas of heavy-duty wear.

Eggshell and Satin

These are finishes that have a little bit of sheen, so they are wonderful choices for walls—they are not so flat that they can't be wiped clean with a damp cloth, but not so shiny that they show off every imperfection. Eggshell is the water-based paint, satin the oil-based version.

Semigloss and High Gloss

These paints give a shiny finish that will highlight any surface flaws. Much more durable and easier to clean, they are good for areas of heavy-duty wear, such as children's rooms and family rooms. The oil-based versions are the most durable and are an obvious choice for woodwork, floors, and moisture-laden kitchens and bathrooms.

Other Finishes

Milk Paint

The oldest form of decorating paint known to man, milk paint is made up of milk proteins, clay, limestone, and earth pigments. It is designed to be used on raw wood surfaces (do not use a primer with milk paint); however, it's not unknown for people to use a rag to rub milk paint very effectively into plaster walls. Milk paint is available in a wide palette of natural, vegetable colors and provides a very authentic colonial look for wood. Just one coat allows the wood tone and grain to show through. For a more opaque finish, sand down the surface of the wood until it is completely smooth and apply two coats.

Milk paint is available at craft and paint stores and comes as a powder that needs to be mixed with water. Follow the manufacturer's instructions to obtain a creamy consistency; use extra water for translucent washes and apply the paint using a foam brush. For stenciling, be sure to use less water than recommended. When choosing milk paint be very certain about your choice; it is virtually impossible to remove. A natural beeswax polish is a perfect sealant for milk-painted surfaces.

Glazes

Glazes combine a pigment with a varnish or sealant to form a translucent topcoat that allows the basecoat to show through. Until recently, the standard has been an oil-based glaze, thinned with a little mineral spirits. However, you can now buy buckets of water-based glaze. To either type of glaze, you can add pigment in the form of paint, tint (see page opposite), or an already-colored glaze to make your own customized colors. Be sure to mix well before you start applying the glaze, and to stir frequently as you work. For a subtle effect, the ratio of color to glaze could be either one to twelve, or one to eight. For a stronger color presence use a ratio of one to four.

Textured Paints

This is a mixture of paint (either water- or oil-based) and sand that produces the look of gritty stucco or rough stone. While it is useful for covering and camouflaging uneven and damaged walls, it is a look that has fallen out of favor, in part because it's so hard to undo.

Acrylic Craft Paints and Artist's Acrylics

Acrylic craft paints, which are water-based, are readily available at craft stores. They come in a plethora of colors in two-ounce bottles. They're very economical, so you can buy lots of colors for stenciling, painting murals, freehand drawing, and to color clear water-based glazes. Artist's acrylics are much the same and also water-based. These come in tubes, rather than bottles, and are thicker—though they can be thinned as needed with water. Both types of paint have fast drying times.

Artist's Oil Paints

Because they dry slowly, you have more time to work with these paints than you do with acrylic paints. These paints come in tubes and, as their name indicates, they are oil-based. Artist's oil paints are useful for finely detailed work: shading areas of a fresco design, painting freehand effects along a wide expanse of soffit, etc.

Japan Paints

Another type of oil-based paint, Japan paints are also available in small quantities. They have a very flat finish but dry much faster than artist's oil paints, making them a wonderful choice for stenciling.

Stencil Creams

These creams are light, water-based paints with a silky, paste-like consistency. They are excellent for novice stencilers because they don't run and will give the soft, understated look that would otherwise take considerable practice and experience to achieve. Stencil creams come in little jars, and are usually applied with foam stencil brushes.

Stains

These are translucent coatings, usually pigmented, for applying to raw wood. The stain will allow the grain of the wood to show through and can alter the color, allowing pine to mimic walnut, golden oak, or even ebony, for example. Stains are also available in many colors in addition to the various wood tones. Some brands include a sealant as well, which will save you from buying and applying a separate product.

Universal Tints and Artist's Tints

These are pure pigment, with no adhesive quality, and therefore can't be used on their own. Instead use them to color paint or glaze—either water-based or oil-

based. They are extremely potent: a tiny bit goes a very long way. The trick is to add the tint drop by drop, stirring in each drop before deciding if more color is desired. This is especially true of black: be very sparing, otherwise you'll find you go from pink directly to dark gray without pausing at mauve.

Crackling Medium

This is brushed on between two layers of paint or glaze and causes the topcoat to crack as it dries, revealing the basecoat beneath. The crackling medium that is sold for home use is water-based and available in one-gallon containers. Many craft and paint stores also carry smaller amounts for use on decorative accessories, as well as kits that include contrasting paints. The chemical composition of the basecoat is not important, but don't paint an oil-based topcoat over water-based crackling medium.

Sealants

These products—varnishes, polyurethanes, acrylic sealers, shellac, and the like—provide a clear, protective outercoat for paint finishes—making the surface more durable. They are all final-step finishes, and are available in varying degrees of sheen: glossy, satin, or matte. Use at least three coats to build up the strongest, most moisture-proof surface. The oil-based products are the most durable but may pick up dust during their slow drying period. They may also yellow over time, though the newer polyurethane varnishes often advertise their nonyellowing formulas. Shellac should be used only over wood.

The Tools

Four-inch brushes: use these to cover large areas. Use the foam or nylon brushes for water-based paints and natural bristle brushes for oil-based paints.

Two-inch slanted brush: invaluable for "cutting in" (see page 184) a line of paint along ceilings and wood trim.

Stencil brushes: these thick, flat brushes should be used in a pouncing or swirling motion. Use foam or nylon bristle for water-based paints, and natural bristle for oil-based paints.

Paint pads: these flat, rectangular pads, with a handle on the back, are for painting along the edges of walls and ceilings and around windows and doors.

A roller and paint tray: use a short piled roller for smooth surfaces, and a thick pile for textured surfaces.

Ragging tools: there is an almost unlimited array of materials and textures that are good for applying and removing paint, such as paper bags and cotton rags (see page 90).

Artist's brushes: extensively used for graphic and figural designs, artist's brushes are also useful for touch-ups.

Sponging tools: natural sea sponges or cellulose kitchen sponges can be used to create a variety of effects. Sponging mitts are also available in craft stores—these are flat oval sponges glued to a cotton mitten (see page 83).

Dragging tools: the classic tool is a stiff, flat brush, but French brushes (which have very short, stiff bristles) and roofer's brushes also produce well-defined striations (see page 111).

Combing tools: the most effective tools are made of slightly flexible rubber. Commercial combs come with standard, regularly spaced teeth, or graduated teeth, and most are multi-sided providing three or four options.

Speckling tools: a toothbrush or stencil brush works fine, though speckling tools are available—small, round brushes with a rotating pin (see page 185).

Other Essentials

Thin rubber gloves, to keep your hands clean

Paint clothes

Dropcloths, old sheets, heavy plastic, and newspaper, for protecting floors and furniture

Spackling compound, for filling holes

Lots of **clean rags**

Painter's tape, for masking

Slats for painting straight edges

Sandpaper in fine, medium, and rough grades, plus a sanding block

Putty knife

Paint scraper

Soft, wide **paintbrush**, for dusting surfaces

Stepladder

Extension handle for rolling ceilings

Metal yardstick, for measuring

Spirit level and **T square**

Preparing Surfaces

First of all, clear and prepare the area; taking away extraneous items, moving furniture away from the walls (or out of the room altogether), taking down window treatments, and removing fixtures and switch plates so far as possible. Use dropcloths to cover the furniture and floor.

For walls that have never been painted

Wallboard, commonly known by the trade name Sheetrock, is used for the vast majority of interior walls in today's homes. Most builders tape the seams, using paper tape and joint compound, and then prime it. If you're doing this job yourself, you need to smooth on the joint compound several times with a putty knife, letting each application dry for a day before continuing. Missed hammer strokes, joints that don't quite fit, and crevices between walls and wood trim, should also receive this plastering process. Once completed, sand down the area to be painted. Brush away any dust from the surface with a wide, soft paintbrush, then vacuum the whole area before starting to paint: to prevent dust from settling on wet paint. Finally, mask off adjacent areas that you don't want painted, and apply a coat of primer to the wall.

For painted wall surfaces

The surface should first be cleaned of dirt and grease. Any mold growth should be destroyed by washing the area a couple of times with a weak bleach and water solution. Allow the area to dry completely before proceeding. Next fill any cracks or holes using a putty knife and spackling compound. Sand and dust the filled areas, then vacuum before priming the surface. (The primer will prevent subsequent coats of paint from soaking into the filled areas and distorting your final finish.) Study the following to see if anything else needs to be done:

1 If the wall to be painted has any sheen, a light sanding with fine sandpaper will scuff the surface, so that subsequent coats of paint will adhere.

2 If you are painting over a darker color than the one you plan to use, apply a primer for easier application of the new paint and better color. Use the criteria above to decide whether the old paint needs to be sanded.

3 Walls with a flat finish and painted in a color that is lighter than the one you're planning will not need to be sanded or primed.

For papered walls

It's rarely a good idea to paint over wallpaper: the seams, the dyes, or the patterns may eventually show through. If the wallpaper is well-adhered to the walls, however, and the walls behind it are crumbly and poor, you may be better off keeping the paper in place. In this case, paper over with liner paper (you can also use this for covering painted walls in poor condition) that can then be painted.

To help strip wallpaper, there are tools that will perforate the paper and machines, available for rent, that force steam under the paper, making it easy to peel off in large sheets. Use a large scraper to start the peeling, and a sanding block to remove stubborn bits of paper. Then lightly sand, dust, and prime the wall before starting your decorative finish. (Don't forget to vacuum before you apply the primer.)

For unpainted wood

Clean and rinse the surface with an all-purpose cleaner. Allow to dry completely, then use sandpaper and steel wool to lightly sand. Fill any holes with caulk or wood filler, sand those areas, vacuum, and prime (unless you are planning to apply a stain or paint with milk paint, both of which should be applied directly to bare wood).

For painted wood

If the existing paint is in poor condition, use paint remover, following the manufacturer's instructions. Then use mineral spirits to remove any residue. If the paint is in good condition, just wash the surface with all-purpose cleaner and allow to dry completely. Then use sandpaper and steel wool to lightly sand the surface. Fill holes with caulk or wood filler, sand those areas, vacuum, then prime. The surface is now ready for painting.

For stained wood without a protective coating

Wipe the surface down with mineral spirits or paint thinner. Then use sandpaper and steel wool to smooth the surface. Fill holes with caulk or wood filler, sand those areas, vacuum, and prime—unless you will be applying another stain or milk paint.

For stained wood with a protective coating

Clean and rinse the surface with an all-purpose cleaner, and allow to dry thoroughly. Use sandpaper and steel wool to smooth the surface. Fill holes with caulk or wood filler, sand those areas, vacuum and prime. Don't apply another stain or milk paint, unless you've had the protective coating professionally stripped.

Finding the Right Color

Once you have a rough idea of the colors you want to use, consult paint chips to refine your choices. You can collect these at any paint store. Study the chips in the area you wish to decorate and match the colors to existing materials. If you are decorating a room, check the chips in the brightest and darkest areas, and in the mix of artificial and natural light.

These days, many paint stores have equipment that can match exact shades. Bear in mind, however, that even the same shade may look different once applied—results depend upon light, the size of the area, and juxtaposed colors. If in doubt, buy the shade you're contemplating in the smallest possible quantity: then paint it onto a small area and consider how it looks when dry, both during the day and at night.

You can also create and mix your own colors at home, though you need to be prepared for a little experimentation. This is all about trial and error—so keep notes about the colors and quantities you are mixing. Otherwise, you'll create just the right color and not know how you did it! You can mix any water-based product with any other water-based product. The same applies to oil-based products. Universal tints can be mixed with both bases—just remember to do this drop by drop.

Quantities

Two coats of paint (excluding the primer) are usually needed to cover a wall or a ceiling adequately. Of course, if the walls are rough or porous, or if you're painting a light color over a dark one, you may need three or more coats.

As a general rule, one gallon of latex paint will cover about 400 square feet, and one gallon of alkyd will cover about 500 square feet; though coverage results vary from product to product, and surface to surface. Always check individual paint cans for more accurate estimates. It's best to overestimate the quantity you'll need; you don't want to run short, and you'll want extra for touch-ups in any case.

For a uniform color, check to ensure the same batch code number is marked on each can. If you end up needing to buy more, "box" your paint: mix the remainder of the first batch into the second, so that any differences in the color are minimized.

If you are using a glaze for the topcoat, you will still need to apply at least two basecoats. A thirty-two-ounce bucket of glaze goes a long way. If you are merely doing a door or two, or some molding, eight ounces will be more than enough.

Applying Paint

With a Brush

For the best finish, use quality brushes designed for the type of paint you are using, i.e., water- or oil-based. For large surfaces use a four-inch brush, and to cut into edges, use a two-inch slanted brush. Foam brushes absorb paints and help to prevent drips, making them great for applying thinner substances, such as stains and glazes that are going to be manipulated with rags, sponges, etc.

To apply the paint, dip the brush into the pot, so that about one-quarter of the bristles are covered. Press the brush against the inside of the pot's rim to remove the excess paint. Then stroke the brush back and forth over the surface. Brush away any drips that form as quickly as possible.

With a Roller

Using a roller means that large, flat surfaces, such as ceilings, walls, and floors, can be covered very quickly. For best results buy a good quality roller with a low pile, unless you are painting a textured surface (or with a textured paint) where the roller will need a high pile. These days some rollers come with all sorts of special features: built-in paint cartridges, pneumatic systems, shields for avoiding any spatters, special extension handles—so you need to weigh the added expense against the necessity for these extras.

Work with a roller in combination with a paint tray. Pour about two-thirds of a cup of paint into the deep well area. Dip the roller into the paint and run it over the ridged, sloping section of the tray to distribute the paint over the entire roller. Then, simply roll the paint onto the surface in crisscrossing diagonal directions. Wear goggles to protect your eyes when you are doing ceilings.

With a Paint Pad

A paint pad is especially handy for edging at the tops of walls and around doors and windows. These are not designed for alkyd paints, so use only with latex. Pour the paint into a shallow pan or paint tray and thin it with a little water. Take care to dip only the pile, and not the backing or edges of the pad, into the paint. Then bring the pad over the pan's edges to remove excess paint. To apply the paint, draw the pad up and down over the surface.

Painting Straight Lines

The ability to paint a neat, straight line is especially necessary where a colored wall meets a white ceiling, where a wall meets molding that won't be painted over afterward, or at any other dividing line that needs to be crisp.

A steady hand can use a two-inch slanted brush to "cut in" the paint. (This brush can also be held sideways for getting into narrow spaces.) Take care to pull the brush smoothly so that one edge of bristles follows the line—this could be an edge or inside corner where two perpendicular surfaces meet. Doing this freehand takes skill, so practice on a scrap of board until you are proficient. You can also make use of paint slats. Hold the slat in place against the surface and paint along it before moving onto the next area.

Probably the best method, however, is to do lots of taping prior to painting. Be sure to burnish the edges of the tape: rub your thumb along the edge to create a tight seal, so that paint won't seep underneath. Painter's tape is preferable to masking tape because it leaves less residue, though you still need to remove the tape promptly. Remove the tape slowly, before the paint has completely dried. Then you will be able to use a single-edge razor blade to carefully scrape away any paint that has bled under the tape. Any other problems, such as smudges or blots, can be touched up later with a small artist's brush.

Stippling

Stippling produces a finely mottled appearance to paint or glaze. The topcoat is applied with a flat brush, and while it is still wet, a stiff brush is pounced in an up-and-down movement over the surface, touching only the ends of the bristles to the surface. Turn the brush as you work to avoid any regularity in the texture and use a rag to intermittently wipe off excess paint from the brush. To cover large surfaces, look for specially designed stipple brushes or consider using a roofing brush.

Speckling or Spattering

This effect can be used to mimic wormholes in wood surfaces, to simulate stone, or to give a free-spirited, dotted look. It is a messy technique, and great care must be taken to mask any adjacent surfaces you don't want spattered. Simply pull a finger through the bristles of an old toothbrush, a stencil brush, or any other small, stiff brush, to lightly and randomly dot the surface. Alternatively, you could use one of the newly available speckling tools (see page 178). Whatever method you decide to use, you have little control over the process, which is part of the spontaneous charm of the results.

Acknowledgments

Country Living would like to thank
the many homeowners, designers, and architects
whose work appears on these pages

PHOTO CREDITS

pages 1 to 19, Keith Scott Morton

page 21, Kari Haavisto

page 22, Keith Scott Morton

pages 24 and 25, Grey Crawford

pages 26 to 28, Keith Scott Morton

page 28, Keith Scott Morton

page 29 center, Keith Scott Morton

page 29 right, Steven Mays

pages 30 to 40, Keith Scott Morton

page 41, Jessie Walker

pages 42 to 60, Keith Scott Morton

page 61, Gus Francisco and Allan Baille

pages 62 and 63, Keith Scott Morton

page 64, Steven Mays

pages 65 to 69, Keith Scott Morton

page 70, Keith Scott Morton

page 71 center, Steven Mays

page 71 right, Keith Scott Morton

page 72, Michael Dunne

page 74, Keith Scott Morton

page 75, Paul Kopelow

pages 76 to 83, Keith Scott Morton

page 84, Jeremy Samuelson

page 85, Steven Mays

pages 86 and 87, Keith Scott Morton

page 88, Paul Kopelow

pages 89 to 93, Keith Scott Morton

page 94, Steven Mays

page 95, Keith Scott Morton

pages 96 to 97, Jeremy Samuelson

pages 98 to 101, Keith Scott Morton

pages 102 to 105, Michael Dunne

pages 106 to 113, Keith Scott Morton

page 114, Steven Mays

pages 116 to 127, Keith Scott Morton

page 128, Lilo Raymond

pages 129 and 130, Keith Scott Morton

page 131, Al Teufen

pages 132 to 145, Keith Scott Morton

page 146 top, Keith Scott Morton

page 146 bottom, Jessie Walker

pages 147 to 151, Keith Scott Morton

pages 152 and 153, Jessie Walker

page 154, Keith Scott Morton

page 155, Jeremy Samuelson

pages 156 to 158, Keith Scott Morton

page 159, Tony Giammarino

page 160, Jessie Walker

page 161, Keith Scott Morton

pages 162 and 163, Peter Vitale

pages 164 to 166, Jessie Walker

page 167, Steven Mays

pages 168 to 192, Keith Scott Morton

Resources

Contact the manufacturers below to locate a retail outlet in your area which carries their products.

ADELE BISHOP DESIGN
3430 South Service Road
Burlington, ON L7N 3T9
Canada
(800) 510-0245
Over 170 pre-cut stencils from historic patterns to contemporary designs, as well as supplies

BENJAMIN MOORE & CO.
51 Chestnut Ridge Road
Montvale, NJ 07645
(800) 826-2623
Interior and exterior paint and stains

BINNEY & SMITH, INC.
1100 Church Lane
Easton, PA 18044-0431
(800) 272-9652
Acrylic paint and artist's brushes

DECOART
PO Box 360
Stanford, KY 40484
(800) 367-3047
Acrylic paint, stencil paint, crackling medium

DELTA TECHNICAL
COATINGS, INC.
2550 Pellissier Place
Whittier, CA 90601-1505
(800) 423-4135
Acrylic paint, crackling medium, stencils and stencil supplies, clear glaze

DURON PAINTS
10406 Tucker Street
Beltsville, MD 20705
(800) 723-8766
Interior and exterior paint

DUTCH BOY PAINT
101 Prospect Avenue
14 Midland Building
Cleveland, OH 44115
(800) 828-5669
Interior and exterior paint

FINNAREN & HALEY, INC.
901 Washington Street
Conshohocken, PA 19428
(800) 843-9800
Interior and exterior paint, including the Colonial Historic Philadelphia and Victorian Hues palettes of authentic colors

FRIENDLY STENCILS
590 King Street
Hanover, MA 02339
(781) 878-7596
Stencils, including authentic patterns from the 1780s to the 1940s, as well as custom-cut designs

THE GLIDDEN CO.
925 Euclid Avenue
Cleveland, OH 44115
(216) 344-8000
Interior and exterior paint, including Spread 2000, a line of non-toxic paint, and The American Collection of historic reproduction colors from the mid-1800s

HELEN FOSTER STENCILS
71 Main Street
Stanford, ME 04073
(207) 490-2625
Specialize in Arts & Crafts–style stencils, wall friezes, and borders from the early 20th century

HISTORIC PAINTS LTD.
Burr Tavern
Route 1, PO Box 474
East Meredith, NY 13757
(607) 431-2311
Specialize in reproducing
authentic 18th- and 19th-
century paint; suppliers of
linseed oil-based paint,
pigments, and water-based
paint

M.A.B. PAINT
(800) 622-1899
Interior and exterior paint,
stains, polyurethanes

MARTHA STEWART PAINT
101 Prospect Avenue
14 Midland Building
Cleveland, OH 44115
(888) 627-8429
Latex paint

MARTIN SEYNOUR PAINT
101 Prospect Avenue
14 Midland Building
Cleveland, OH 44115
(800) 677-5270
Interior and exterior paint
and accessories

THE OLD-FASHIONED
MILK PAINT COMPANY
PO Box 222
436 Main Street
Groton, MA 01450-0222
(508) 448-6336
Milk paint

OMNIGRID, INC.
1560 Port Drive
Burlington, WA 98233
(360) 757-4743
Clear quilter's rulers, triangles

PLAID ENTERPRISES, INC.
1649 International Court
PO Box 7600
Norcross, GA 30091-7600
(770) 923-8200
Clear and colored glazes,
acrylic paint, stamps, crackling
medium, antiquing medium
and antiquing wash, stencils,
and general supplies

PRATT & LAMBERT PAINTS
101 Prospect Avenue
14 Midland Building
Cleveland, OH 44115
(800) 289-7728
Interior and exterior paint,
stains, custom color matching

RALPH LAUREN PAINT
101 Prospect Avenue
14 Midland Building
Cleveland, OH 44115
(800) 379-7656
Interior paint, unique finishes,
crackling medium, stencil sets

SHERWIN WILLIAMS CO.
101 Prospect Avenue
14 Midland Building
Cleveland, OH 44115
(800) 474-3794
Interior and exterior paint
and accessories

THE STENCIL COLLECTOR &
STENCIL LIBRARY
1723 Tilghman Street
Allentown, PA 18104
(610) 433-2105
Specialize in period stencil
designs from England; as well
as supplies

TULIP
24 Prime Park Way
Natick, MA 01760
(800) 458-7010
Milk paint

YOWLER & SHEPPS STENCILS
3529 Main Street
Conestoga, PA 17516
(717) 872-2820
Original stencil patterns
inspired by English and French
country designs, as well as
supplies

Index